Curie

for Katie

Curie

Sarah Dry

with an essay by Sabine Seifert

HAUS PUBLISHING · LONDON

First published in Great Britain in 2003 by
Haus Publishing Limited
32 Store Street
London WC1E 7BS

A CIP catalogue record for this book
is available from the British Library

ISBN 1-904341-29 2 (paperback)

Designed and typeset in Albertina at Libanus Press, Marlborough

Printed and bound by Graphicom in Vicenza, Italy

Front cover: photograph of Marie Curie courtesy of Association
Curie et Joliot-Curie
Back cover: caricature of Marie and Pierre Curie courtesy of
Ann Ronan Picture Library

Contents

Early Years · 1867–1891

Marie Curie was born Manya Skłodowska in Warsaw on 7 November 1867. The last of five children born to schoolteacher parents, she entered a world of daily indignities. Her family, her language, and her culture were proudly Polish, but Poland officially did not exist. Once the largest nation in Europe, it had been progressively partitioned by Russia, Austria, and Prussia throughout the 18th century until it ceased to exist as an independent state in 1795. Of the three foreign powers occupying the nation, Russia was the most oppressive, dominating Warsaw and the eastern territories. Just four years before Manya was born, Poles had mounted an unsuccessful rebellion. The Russian response was brutal. Thousands of Poles were imprisoned, exiled, or sent to Siberian work camps; the Russian viceroy was installed in the former residence of the Polish monarch; Polish street signs and the teaching of Polish history and language were strictly forbidden.

Manya's parents, Wladislaw and Bronislawa Skłodowski, belonged to a liberal, modestly intellectual community in Warsaw. Despite the Russian laws forbidding it, they taught secret classes in Polish language and history at considerable risk to themselves and their pupils. The harsh response to the 1863 uprising had quashed any hopes of Polish self-rule in the near future, but it did not eradicate the Polish resistance movement. Though Manya's parents were far from radical, they pursued a uniquely Polish form of defiance: education offered hope for the future.

For the young Manya Skłodowska, family life and schooling were tightly bound. Her parents imbued their daughter with a lasting belief in the transforming values of study and of patience. Manya's father, Wladislaw, taught physics and mathematics in a government-run school, hounded by Russian supervisors keen to detect any subversive teaching. His fastidious demeanour, later described by his granddaughter Eve Curie as that of 'the perfect government official',[1] may have been a professional necessity to avoid conflict with aggressive overseers. Bronislawa taught and managed a small private school for girls, which escaped the constant scrutiny of the boys-only government schools but was still subject to surprise visits from the Russian inspector. It was at her mother's school that Manya was born. Her intelligence quickly became apparent. By four, she surprised her parents by reading entire sentences effortlessly. In primary school, the teacher relied on Manya during visits from the school inspector. The students quickly hid their contraband Polish history books. The young Manya, terrified of the inspector, was nonetheless able to recite the required litany of the Tsars in perfect Russian.

The Skłodowskis led a comfortable if not luxurious life until 1873, when the family's fortunes took a decided turn for the worse. Wladislaw was dismissed from his post at the government school. Forced to take in boarders, the Skłodowski family lived amid a cacophony of nearly 20 young students. Their new lodgers studied in all parts of the house, lunched with

Manya's mother, Bronislawa Skłodowska

the family, and ultimately, perhaps, contributed to the first tragedy of Manya's youth, the death of her eldest sister Zosia of typhoid in 1876, when Manya was just nine. Zosia's death weakened an already ailing Bronislawa. Just two years later, in 1878, Manya's mother died of tuberculosis. The diminished family unit now comprised Manya, her father, her sisters Bronia and Helena, and her brother Józef.

Bronislawa's death devastated Manya and her family. Many years later, Curie would write: *This catastrophe was the first great sorrow of my life and threw me into a profound depression. My mother had an exceptional personality. With all her intellectuality she had a big heart and a very high sense of duty. And, though possessing infinite indulgence and good nature, she still held in the family a remarkable moral authority.*[2]

In 1878, barely 11 years old and just a few months after her mother's death, Manya set out for Gymnasium Number Three, a Russian-run school where the Polish language was forbidden and the teaching was patchy at best. Manya felt that the teachers were *hostile to the Polish nation* and that *the moral atmosphere was altogether unbearable.*[3] But her attitude shifted during her four years at the gymnasium. At the end of her time there she wrote to her close friend Kazia that *In spite of everything, I like school.*[4] Like her brother Józef and sister Bronia before her, she graduated with the gold medal for first place.

Manya was the distinguished product of a system that had nothing more to offer her. Formal schooling for girls in Poland ended at age 15. Marriage was the next

The Skłodowskis in 1890: from left to right, Manya, Wladislaw, Bronia and Helena. (Józef is not pictured.)

DEATH OF MOTHER

step for many. Manya was still too young, and with a wilful temperament that made her a less than likely candidate for an early marriage. Watching her parents, she had learned that it was worth fighting an oppressive system, even if there seemed little immediate hope for change. Though she was disadvantaged, both as a woman and as a Pole, she was resolved not to settle for an ordinary life. She was not yet certain what form her life would take, but her ideas did not include an early marriage or an education that stopped at age 15. Before Manya could decide what path would best suit her as yet unformed ambition, she took a year out to recover, as she put it, *from the fatigue of growth and study*. Her year of rest included visits to several relatives living in the Polish countryside, where there were plenty of distractions for a young woman, and is an early example of what would become a common pattern in Curie's life of intense work followed by exhaustion.

Manya's letters of the time show her discovering a girlish excitement that had eluded her in the sad Warsaw household of her father. *I have been to a kulig,* she writes to Kazia of a traditional Polish sleigh party, itself a sign of resistance to Russian cultural domination. *You can't imagine how delightful it is, especially when the clothes are beautiful and the boys are well dressed. My costume was very pretty . . . After this first kulig there was another, at which I had a marvellous time. There were a great many young men from Cracow, very handsome boys who danced so well! It is altogether exceptional to find such good dancers. At eight o'clock in the morning we danced the last dance – a white mazurka.*[5]

'THESE GIFTS MUST NOT DISAPPEAR'

A year of mazurkas would have to suffice for a lifetime. This period of carefree pleasure was the last time Manya would be without responsibilities and without the pressure her own ambition created. In late summer, she returned to Warsaw. Her only opportunity for further education was the 'Floating University', an underground academy that held secret classes in living rooms and meeting halls. Manya was one of more than a thousand young women who continued their studies in this way. During this period she read widely in French, German, Russian, and Polish, absorbing the *Fables* of Jean de La Fontaine, the poems of Heinrich Heine, the novels of Dostoevsky, and Ernest Renan's seminal sceptical reading of the gospels, *Life of Jesus*, all in their original languages.

Attending the Floating University meant opposing Russian rule. Its clandestine setting and educational mission epitomized the ethos of the Polish resistance movement. Manya's fellow students believed that study, rather than armed insurrection, would lay the necessary groundwork for future freedom. This Polish manifestation of Auguste Comte's philosophy of 'positivism' infused the informal Floating University, and the diffuse resistance movement of which it formed a part. Polish positivists advocated incremental change rather than revolutionary ruptures as the best way to solve the entrenched political problems facing the former Polish nation in the late 19th century. 'We believe neither in revolution nor in radical utopias which profess to change society overnight and to cure all its social ills', wrote Polish positivist Józef Kraszewski. 'We believe in slow and gradual progress [which] through reforming individuals, increasing enlightenment, encouraging work, order and moderation should accomplish the most salutary revolution, or rather evolution in the social system.'[6]

Though she understood the need to be patient and work hard, Manya, like many others, dreamed of leaving Warsaw to pursue further education in Paris, the most modern city of the time and one with a decades-long tradition of welcoming Polish exiles. As a young woman, she could not earn enough money on her own to pay for the three-day journey to Paris, much less her school fees and living expenses once she got there. So she and her sister Bronia hatched a plan: if they pooled their resources, one sister could work

As schoolgirls, Manya Skłodowska and her best friend Kazia walked across Saxony Square in Warsaw every day and pause to spit as they passed the 'pompous obelisk' dedicated by the Russian Tsar 'To the Poles Faithful to their Sovereign'. Warsaw was a city with two faces at the time of Manya's childhood. Beneath a surface loyalty to Russian rule the Polish citizens expressed their dissatisfaction. Many Poles in this period advocated a philosophy derived from the positivism of the Frenchman Auguste Comte (1798–1857). Comte had coined the term positivism to describe a new secular 'religion of humanity' that he envisioned leading mankind away from metaphysical and theological thinking towards a rational, law-based moral system. Polish positivists kept the name and the belief in practical means and transformed the rigid French philosophy into an eminently useable doctrine, part political strategy, part coping mechanism. This pragmatic creed offered a way of enduring the harsh reality of newly severe Russian domination following the failed rebellion of 1863. The romantic idealism that had spurred the Poles to direct rebellion no longer served: 'The ideals of the past,' declared the positivist leader Aleksander Swietochowski, 'are not the ideals of the present.'[7] For Polish positivists, the ideal form of resistance to the Russians was steady work and education. As it turned out, these were ideals that suited Manya perfectly. The anger of the girl who spat at Russian monuments fed the fearsome focus and drive of the young student. Her future scientific work would be guided by her belief in proceeding in an orderly, well-founded, and cohesive manner. She called it the creed of 'disinterestedness': setting lofty goals and working towards them with a steady disregard for mundane distractions.

to help send the other to Paris to pursue further education and then the other could follow. Manya, being younger, would have to wait. First, she would take a job as a governess: in exchange for room and board and a stipend, she would tutor the young children of a middle-class Polish family. Living in a rural community, with all her expenses paid, she would be able to save far more than she could as a tutor in Warsaw. She would use her earnings to help send her older sister to Paris. Bronia, who planned to become a doctor, would send for Manya when she had saved enough money. It was a laborious solution, but it was the only way either of them could see out of a middling life in an oppressed country.

The sisters put their plan into action as soon as possible. In 1886, 19-year-old Manya found a position as governess to the Zorawskis, a prosperous sugar-beet farming family. Manya found the rural outpost, surrounded by miles of sugar beets, to be less than stimulating. Her letters home reveal an already astute mind taking the measure of her rural peers. *They are not bad creatures, for that matter, and certain ones are even intelligent but their education has done nothing to develop their minds, and the stupid, incessant parties here have ended by frittering their wits away. As for the young men, there are few nice ones who are even a bit intelligent . . . For the girls and boys alike, such words as 'positivism' or 'the labour question' are objects of aversion – supposing they have ever heard the words, which is unusual.*[8] To her friend Henrietta, who had written with news of politics back home, she wrote: *It is a real satisfaction for me to learn that there exist some regions and some geographic areas in which people move and even think. While you are living at the centre of the movement, my existence strangely resembles that of one of those slugs which haunt the dirty water of our river. Luckily I hope to get out of this lethargy soon.*[9]

Manya (left) and her sister Bronia in 1886

Manya continued alone the wide-ranging study she had begun at the Floating University, reading such important recent books as Alfred Daniel's *Physics*, Herbert Spencer's *Sociology* in French and Paul Ber's *Lessons on Anatomy and Physiology* in German. Her tastes were catholic enough at first, but she came to understand during her time in the country that it was the physical sciences that offered

GOVERNESS IN THE COUNTRY

the analytical puzzles and the opportunity for disciplined laboratory work that truly interested her. Years later she would write,
*Literature interested me as much as sociology and science. Still, during these
years of work, as I tried gradually to discover my true preferences, I finally
turned towards mathematics and physics.*[10] Manya yearned to do experimental work and complained of the lack of laboratory in a letter
to her brother Józef. *Think of it: I am learning chemistry from a book.
You can imagine what little I get out of that, but what can I do, as I have no
place to make experiments, or do practical work?*[11]

Though Manya was passionate about her private studies and
dreamt of greater self-fulfilment in Paris, she was not immune
to her immediate surroundings. Despite her bookishness and
her occasional brooding, she fell in love with her employer's
son, Kazimierz Zorawski. The affair ended in disappointment.
Kazimierz, unwilling to go against his parents' wishes for a more
appropriate match, rejected Manya. The end of the relationship,
which must have started during
one of Kazimierz's school holidays, put Manya into a despairing
frame of mind. Her plans began
to seem overly ambitious and
doomed to fail. She wrote plain-
tively to her brother, *now that I have
lost the hope of ever becoming anybody,
all my ambition has been transferred to
Bronia and you. You two, at least, must
direct your lives according to your gifts.
These gifts, which, without any doubt,
do exist in our family, must not disappear ... The more regret I have for
myself the more hope I have for you.*[12]

Kazimierz Zorawski

Manya distracted herself by

tutoring local peasant children who crowded into her room on Wednesdays and Saturdays for up to five hours of teaching at a time. She fulfilled the remaining two years of her contract with a bitter determination until, now 22 years old, she returned to her father's house in Warsaw to take up a position as a local governess and to resume her classes at the Floating University. At this point she had her first encounter with a modest laboratory run by a cousin named Józef Boguski. The oddly named 'Museum of Industry and Agriculture' was really an ill-equipped but serviceable laboratory where Poles could be taught science away from prying Russian eyes. It was an experience that, however limited, helped to steer Manya towards her ultimate vocation. *To my great joy, I was able, for the first time in my life, to find access to a laboratory: a small municipal physical laboratory directed by one of my cousins. I found little time to work there, except in the evenings and on Sundays, and was generally left to myself. I tried out various experiments described in treatises on physics and chemistry, and the results were sometimes unexpected. At times I would be encouraged by a little unhoped-for success, at others I would be in the deepest despair because of accidents and failures resulting from my inexperience. But on the whole, though I was taught that the way of progress is neither swift nor easy, this first trial confirmed in me the taste for experimental research in the fields of physics and chemistry.*[13]

Meanwhile, Bronia had been attending medical school in Paris. In 1890, four years after they had originally made their plan, Bronia wrote to say that she was engaged to a fellow medical student, named Kazimierz Dluski. 'If everything goes as we hope, I shall surely be able to marry when the [summer] holidays begin. My fiancé will be a doctor by then, and I shall have only my last examination to pass . . . And now you, my little Manya: you must make something of your life sometime. If you can get together a few hundred rubles this year you can come to Paris next year and live with us, where you will find board and lodging . . . You must take this decision; you have been waiting too long.'[14] At the last minute, Manya hesitated, struck perhaps with a fear of facing what she had for so long imagined and intermittently despaired of achieving. *Dear Bronia, I have been stupid, I am stupid and I shall remain stupid all the days of my life, or rather, to translate into the current style: I have never been, am not, and shall never be lucky. I dreamed of Paris as of redemption, but the hope of going there left me long ago. And now that the possibility is offered me, I do not know what to do . . . I am afraid to speak of it to Father: I believe our plan of living together next year is close to his heart, and he clings to it; I want to give him a little happiness in his old age. On the other hand, my heart breaks when I think of ruining my abilities, which must have been worth, anyhow, something.*[15]

She wrote this anguished letter in March 1890. It would be more than a year before she could bring herself to leave her father and her home. She spent the summer in the Tatra mountains, recuperating from a sickness that coincided with the long-awaited opportunity to go to Paris. 'Your invitation to Paris which fell upon her in such unexpected fashion,' a worried Wladislaw wrote Bronia, 'has given her a fever and added to her disorder. I feel the power with which she wills to approach that source of science, towards which she aspires so much.' By September, Manya had pulled herself around: *Now Bronia, I ask you for a definite answer. Decide if you can really take me in at your home, for I can come now . . . I am so nervous at the prospect of my departure that I can't speak of anything else until I get your answer.*[16] Bronia's answer was as expected. She urged Manya to come with enough money to enrol in classes at the Sorbonne and with her own bedding and linen, to save on additional expenses. In November 1891, Manya left for Paris in a bare fourth-class railway carriage.

Paris · 1891–1897

RADISHES AND CHERRIES

The Manya Skłodowska who arrived in Paris in the autumn of 1891 was a plumpish 24-year-old with wispy blond hair and a supply of high-necked, long-sleeved floor-length dresses. As a governess and young student in Warsaw, she had proven herself to be confident, motivated, and given to occasional spells of gloominess and despair. She had thoroughly imbibed the values of study and patience taught in the Skłodowska home, and had a firm sense of her own not inconsiderable talents.

She took to Paris immediately. It was an exciting place to be, perhaps the most exciting city in the world at the time. Just two years earlier, the Eiffel Tower had been completed and had received two

million visitors during the Paris Exposition of 1889. Spectacular shopping arcades tempted newly self-aware consumers with what would have been, just ten years earlier, unimaginable variety. Poets, artists, and political radicals smoked cigarettes and argued at already famous cafés.

But though she may have been impressed by her novel surroundings, she was not daunted by them. After years of living as a servant in other people's homes, she revelled in her new-found independence. She stayed with her sister Bronia and brother-in-law Kazimierz only briefly before moving to her own garret apartment in the Latin Quarter, closer to the classrooms, laboratories, and libraries of the Sorbonne. While Bronia's house had provided a gentle transition into France, a Polish home-away-from-home, it had a disadvantage: Kazimierz was inveterately sociable. Once she had moved out, Manya would write to her brother Józef with relief: *I am working a thousand times as hard as at the beginning of my stay: in the rue d'Allemagne my little brother-in-law had the habit of disturbing me endlessly. He absolutely could not endure having me do anything but engage in agreeable chatter with him when I was home. I had to declare war on him on this subject.*[17]

Manya moved to a cheap student flat – the six flights of stairs, the water that froze in the washbasin, and her meals of bread, chocolate, eggs, and fruit all seemed to suit her. Her studiousness, stifled by Russian-dominated schools and years of teaching other people's children, was finally free to express itself fully. Sometimes she became so absorbed in her study that she forgot to eat. At one point her absent-mindedness got the better of her and she fainted. On being questioned by the irritated and no doubt worried Kazimierz, she revealed that she had eaten only radishes and cherries in the past 24 hours.

Biographies of Curie have made much of her straitened circumstances in her early years in Paris. But, though it is true that she lived a life of privation during her four years as a student at the Sorbonne, surviving on just three francs a day, many other foreign students were in similar situations. Equally, her penchant for solitude, much referred to by biographers and by Curie herself, was tempered by the attractions of a lively student ex-patriot community. These students were, like Manya, the most motivated and ambitious their respective countries had to offer. They came to Paris to seek the opportunities that politics or custom denied

When Manya was studying there in the last years of the 19th century, the Sorbonne was a vibrant research university, but it had not always been so. When the revolution came in 1789, the Sorbonne's links to the establishment made it distinctly unpopular and it fell into disregard and disuse for much of the 19th century. It was not until France's quick and decisive defeat in the Franco-Prussian war of 1870–71 that the country's educational system was overhauled. Attributing the Germans' military might to a superior system of education, especially in science, French leaders set about improving science schooling at home. The Sorbonne was the central feature of this educational revolution. The university's old clerical ideals were replaced with newly secular and expressly rational principles and a major rebuilding project was undertaken, including the creation of deluxe new classrooms and state-of-the-art laboratories. The science faculty doubled in size between 1876 and 1900 as bright young faculty members were hired to do original research, teach practical laboratory courses, and oversee informal seminars.

them at home. In this atmosphere, Manya's presence as a foreigner and a woman was not as strange as we might imagine. While foreigners, and especially women, made up a small percentage of the student population – of over 1,800 students enrolled in the Faculty of Sciences in 1891, Manya was one of only 23 women – they occupied a particular and recognized niche. It is a curious fact that of the early doctoral degrees in science awarded to women at the Sorbonne (of which Curie was to receive the first in physical sciences), the lion's share went to women with foreign surnames. Manya was unique in her persistence and the degree of her success, but she belonged to a community of Poles, Americans, and Eastern Europeans with a shared desire to use the open-mindedness of the French Third Republic to realize their dreams. Ironically, French women were more under-represented at the university. While the state was ideologically committed to equality in education, the bourgeois families who could afford to send their daughters to the Sorbonne often preferred to educate them in the domestic, as opposed to liberal, arts.

In later years, Marie Curie would recall as *one of the best memories of my life that period of solitary years exclusively devoted to the studies, finally within my reach, for which I had waited so long.*[18] In none of her reminiscences does she mention what it was like to be a woman in the male-dominated world of the Sorbonne, where, until shortly before her arrival, the word for female student, *étudiante*, had referred to the mistress of a male student. And when she mentions the privations of poor student life, she quickly emphasizes the *very precious sense of liberty and independence*[19] she had gained. *All that I saw and learned that was new delighted me. It was like a new world opened to me, the world of science, which I was at last permitted to know in all liberty.*[20] In accord with this freedom, and signalling a willingness to embrace the culture to which she was fast adapting, Manya registered at the university under a new name: Marie Skłodowska.

Despite her years of hard work in Poland, Marie found herself relatively unprepared for the difficult coursework. She buckled down to study and lab work and abandoned the companionship of the small colony of Polish students. *I was forced to give up these relationships, for I found that all my energy had to be concentrated on my studies, in order to achieve them as soon as possible.*[21] She studied under some of the best physicists and mathematicians in France, including Gabriel Lippmann, who would win a Nobel Prize in 1908 for his work on colour photography, Paul Appell, who would go on to head the Faculty of Sciences, and Henri Poincaré, the great mathematician and physicist who created the study of topology in mathematics and did important work in celestial dynamics, founding the modern theory of dynamical systems. Marie's years of study were rewarded spectacularly when, in 1893, she took first place in the examination for the *licence* (roughly equivalent to a master's degree) in physical sciences, one of just two women awarded the degree in all of the university.

Marie had tasted the sweetness of success and of open access to the laboratories and knowledge she had yearned for in Poland. But her homeland continued to exert a powerful pull on her, as it would for her entire life. Every summer she returned home to Warsaw, and from there travelled with her family in Poland and Switzerland. After Marie's first triumph on the physical sciences exam, a Polish friend, Jadwiga Dydńska, arranged a 600-ruble Alexandrovitch scholarship that enabled Marie to return to Paris to pursue a second degree in mathematics. Marie's letter to her brother on her return to school in the autumn of 1893 captures her excitement and her need to justify her distance from her family, particularly her widowed father. *I hardly need say that I am delighted to be back in Paris . . . And as for me, it is my whole life that is at stake. It seemed to me, therefore, that I could stay on here without having remorse on my conscience.*[22]

'A TALL YOUNG MAN WITH AUBURN HAIR AND LARGE, LIMPID EYES'

Marie had always intended to return to Poland after finishing her studies in Paris. She felt a duty to contribute to her country, and, perhaps more acutely, to care for her ageing father. But in the spring of 1894, she met Pierre Curie, *a tall young man with auburn hair and large, limpid eyes*[23] at the home of physicist and fellow Pole, Józef Zowalski. Thirty years after their first meeting, Marie still remembered it vividly. *As I entered the room, Pierre Curie was standing in the recess of a French window opening on a balcony. He seemed to me very young, though he was at that time 35 years old. I was struck by the open expression of his face and by the slight suggestion of detachment in his whole attitude.*

Pierre Curie

MEETING PIERRE

His speech, rather slow and deliberate, his simplicity, and his smile, at once grave and youthful, inspired confidence. Marie understood Pierre's detachment as that of a *dreamer absorbed in his reflections.*[24]

To Marie, for whom a studied disregard for everyday discomforts was becoming something of a creed, Pierre's natural calm was attractive, his aloofness alluring. Pierre seems to have lived a life apart, heedless of the conventions by which other people lived. Even in his early years, Pierre's family had noted his difficulty in shifting rapidly between subjects and his need to absorb a topic in isolation. Instead of forcing him to adapt to the requirements of a normal curriculum, his family had found ways to foster his special brand of intelligence. He was kept out of the rigid French educational system and was taught at home until the age of 16 by his parents, his elder brother, and a tutor. Pierre thrived, receiving his bachelor's degree at 16 and a *licence* in physics from the Sorbonne just two years later. He stayed at the Sorbonne for five years as an assistant in the laboratory of Paul Desains, the

Pierre Curie undoubtedly inherited much of his aversion to special honours and his loyalty to science from his father, who had lived according to unpopular ideals. Eugène Curie (1827–1910) was a doctor and a radical who espoused anticlericalism and egalitarianism during what were in France the tumultuous middle decades of the 19th century. He participated directly in the 1848 revolution, where he was wounded by government troops, and in the 1871 uprising against the government in Versailles, when he turned his Parisian apartment into an emergency clinic. Himself the son of a doctor-revolutionary, Eugène Curie created a household in which religion and formality had no place. A relaxed family portrait (on facing page) of Eugène, his wife Sophie-Claire, Jacques and Pierre Curie reveals a group of knowing, very individual personalities. Sophie-Claire, wearing a highly patterned dress, looks up with a wry smile from her knitting. Eugène wears a peasant's straw hat and has one arm hooked over the back of his chair. Jacques presents his profile to the camera, staring dramatically to the side. Pierre rests his elbow on Jacques' shoulder in an attitude of thoughtfulness and easy-going fraternity.

The Curie family. Clockwise from top left: Jacques, Pierre, his father Eugene, and mother Sophie

director of the university laboratory, gaining experience in experimental research, though he was unable to carry out any further formal studies for lack of funds.

Though he enjoyed the atmosphere and the challenges of the physics laboratory, Pierre was unusually sensitive to distractions and craved solitude. At 20 he recorded his frustration in a diary entry: 'When, in the process of turning slowly upon myself, I try to gain momentum, a nothing, a word, a story, a paper, a visit stops me and is able to put off or retard for ever the moment when, granted a sufficient swiftness I might have, in spite of my surroundings, concentrated on my own intention ... We must eat, drink, sleep, be idle, love, touch the sweetest things of life and yet not succumb to them. It is necessary that, in doing all this, the higher thoughts to which one is dedicated remain dominant and continue their unmoved course in our poor heads. It is necessary to make a dream of life, and to make of a dream a reality.'[25] This was Pierre's vision of the anti-natural life, as he called it, a life consecrated to a higher ideal.

PIERRE'S IDEALS

Before he met Marie, Pierre's closest relationships were with his parents, with whom he still lived at age 35, and his brother Jacques, his elder by three and a half years. Like Pierre, Jacques had been educated outside the formal French system. He too was drawn to the sciences, working as an assistant in the mineralogical laboratory at the Sorbonne. They pooled their interests in a study of crystals that quickly led to the discovery of piezoelectricity, a remarkable phenomenon that would serve Marie Curie well in the coming years.

The brothers had started with a simple question: what exactly makes a crystal symmetrical? A careful experimental programme designed to answer this basic question uncovered a surprising effect. Because of their regular molecular structure, certain crystals generate an electric current when compressed and the strength of the current depends precisely on the degree of compression. (The effect works in reverse as well: applying a current to a crystal causes it to change shape slightly.) Pierre and Jacques Curie, 21 and 24 years old respectively, were the first to notice and test this phenomenon. They quickly realized that this peculiar property, which they named piezoelectricity, had interesting practical applications, particularly with certain types of crystal, such as quartz. The brothers designed a device, named a piezoelectric quartz electrometer, that could be used to measure tiny amounts of electricity more precisely than had ever been possible before. Their invention would later provide the basis for sensitive sonar equipment, the spark generators in electronic igniters, the buzzers used in mobile phones and pagers, and the inexpensive but highly accurate timekeeping mechanism used in quartz watches.

Despite the Curie brothers' close and productive relationship, their collaboration ended in 1883 when Jacques became head lecturer in Mineralogy at the University of Montpellier. At the same time, Pierre became director of laboratory work at the *École*

Municipale de Physique et Chimie Industrielle (Municipal College of Physics and Industrial Chemistry), EPCI hereafter, a recently founded Parisian vocational school. He was just 24 years old. He would spend the next 22 years of his life at the EPCI's complex of buildings on rue Lhomond, twelve of them as director of lab work and the following ten as professor of physics. There is no doubt that Pierre's unorthodox education and his aversion to convention had an impact on his career. When he met Marie at the age of 35, he had never bothered to fulfil the formal requirements for a doctorate, though he had completed original work on crystal symmetry, magnetism, and precision measurement instrumentation, any portion of which would have sufficed to earn him the degree.

'HYPNOTIZED BY OUR DREAMS'

Pierre did not neglect the formalities of courtship with Marie. Her serious personality, fair features, and plain dress accorded well with his view of life. Unlike some pairings, which thrive on the frisson of difference, the relationship that grew between Marie and Pierre Curie seems to have been founded from the start on shared interests and a common ethical code. Following their initial meeting (one senses that it must have been a set-up arranged by Marie's friend Zowalski), Marie and Pierre became friends, spending time together at the Parisian Physics Society, in the laboratory, and in her student rooms. In the spring of 1894, Marie completed her second *licence* degree at the Sorbonne, placed second out of all students applying for the degree in mathematics. By mid-summer, when Marie left for her customary holiday in Poland, Pierre had expressed his desire to share his life with her. If Marie preferred, as he suggested in one letter, he would be content to occupy separate rooms in a shared flat. Marie was deeply divided. She had finished the degrees she had come to Paris to obtain, and felt obliged to care for her father, and contribute to a still-oppressed Poland. She returned home unsure of her plans, leaving Pierre the task of convincing a headstrong young woman to return to Paris, and to him, in the autumn.

Pierre sent Marie love letters that she would remember fondly 30 years later. He knew Marie well enough to avoid the sentiments of ordinary romance. He cast his plea for Marie to return to Paris in loftier terms, which reveal his astute study of Marie and her jostling passions. 'It would be a fine thing,' he wrote, 'in which I hardly dare believe, to pass our lives near each other, hypnotized by our dreams: *your* patriotic dream, *our* humanitarian dream, and *our* scientific dream. Of all those dreams that last is, I believe, the only legitimate one. I mean by that that we are powerless to change the social order and, even if we were not, we should not know what to do; in taking action, no matter in what direction, we should never be sure of not doing more harm than good, by retarding some inevitable evolution. From the scientific point of view, on the contrary, we may hope to do something; the ground is solider here, and any discovery that we make, however small, will remain acquired knowledge.'[26]

For 26-year-old Marie it was a decision full of anguish. She worried that returning to Paris would allow her dream of an independent Poland, and her own Polishness, to die. Her brother wrote to assure her this was not the case. 'I think you are right to follow your heart, and no just person can reproach you for it. Knowing you, I am convinced that you will remain Polish with all your soul, and also that you will never cease to be part of our family in your heart. And we, too, will never cease to love you and consider you ours. I would infinitely rather see you in Paris, happy and contented, than back again in our country, broken by the sacrifice of a whole life and victim of a too subtle conception of your duty.'[27]

Marie decided to stay in Paris. In a letter to her old friend Kazia, Marie resolutely outlined the bounds of her new life in blunt

Pierre's favourite picture of Marie, looking like 'the good little student', as he called her

sentences that underline the distance between the young girl who had left Poland three years earlier and the grown woman living and now marrying abroad. *It is a sorrow to me to have to stay for ever in Paris, but what am I to do? Fate has made us deeply attached to each other and we cannot endure the idea of separating . . . I hesitated for a whole year and could not resolve upon an answer. Finally I became reconciled to the idea of settling here. When you receive this letter, write to me: Madame Curie, School of Physics and Chemistry, 42 rue Lhomond. That is my name from now on. My husband is a teacher in that school. Next year I shall bring him to Poland so that he will know my country.*[28] In July 1895, just over a year since they had first met, she and Pierre were married in a simple ceremony at the town hall in Sceaux, the suburb of

MARRIAGE

Paris where Pierre's parents lived. Marie wore a navy-blue suit, happy at the presence of her father, her sisters Bronia and Helena, and her brother-in-law Kazimierz.

The newlyweds celebrated with a 'wedding tramp', riding about the Île-de-France (a region of northern France) on freshly purchased bicycles. They rode in the countryside around Paris, hiked through muddy forests, slept in simple country inns and settled into the reality of a life spent wholly together. As they explored a wild wood, with little more than a compass and some fruit, they discussed the wonders of the world revealed by Pierre's experiments with crystals or by the abundance of wildlife in a hidden pond surrounded by reeds. Pierre surprised a dozing Marie by placing a frog in her hand, causing the otherwise stalwart scientist to shriek like a child. In spite of this incident, their shared love of nature would serve as an additional bond in their very close and exclusive relationship.

By October they had settled back into life in Paris in a little three-room flat at 24, rue de la Glacière, whose sparse furnishings were duly noted in the expenses book that Marie began on their return. Pierre had finally gathered his writings on magnetism and presented them for examination for a doctorate. The degree was soon granted and Pierre was appointed professor at EPCI, freeing him from some of the administrative duties that had taken up much of his time and giving him a salary more suited to married life. Marie meanwhile was busily pursuing research into the magnetic properties of steel at high temperatures, having received an industrial grant to do so. She was also studying for the *agrégation*, a qualification that would enable her to teach at a girls' secondary school and so bring in additional income to the household. Salaried research opportunities for a female scientist were nonexistent.

Marie took the exam for the *agrégation* in July 1896. She came first

Pierre and Marie with their beloved bicycles in 1895, the year they were married

in her class; her reward was a bicycle trip in Auvergne with Pierre. It was a breathlessly happy time, as Marie remembered later: *A radiant memory remains from one sunny day when, after a long and difficult ascent, we traversed the fresh green fields of Aubrac in the pure air of the high plateau. Another living memory is that of an evening when, loitering at dusk in the gorges of the Truyère, we were particularly taken by a folk-song dying away in the distance, sung on a boat that was going down the current of the water. Having planned our stages badly, we could not get back to our lodging before dawn: a meeting with some carts whose horses were frightened at our bicycles made us cut across the tilled fields. We took the road afterwards across the high plateau bathed in the unreal light of the moon, while the cows who were passing the night in enclosures came to contemplate us gravely with their great, tranquil eyes.*[29] Marie worked with driven intensity.

But on her holidays she could open herself to the calmer pleasures of the world around her.

During her early married life, Marie managed the household finances, cooked, decorated the house (albeit in a very limited way), and mended clothes, all while studying and pursuing her research into the magnetic properties of steel. Though Pierre was eager to share laboratory work with Marie, he seems to have been less eager to share in the housework. She learned to leave stews to simmer during the morning while she studied, ready for the midday meal. And she planned the simple furnishings in their flat to keep *to a style which gives me no worries and will not require attention, as I have very little help: a woman who comes for an hour a day to do the heavy work. I do the cooking and housekeeping myself.*[30] Marie never questioned her right to participate in the male-dominated worlds of the university and the laboratory, but she also did not question her obligation to shoulder the traditional domestic responsibilities of a wife.

By the beginning of 1897, Marie was pregnant with her first child. From the start, her attitude towards motherhood was unusual. Instead of the bed rest that marked the pregnancies of many upper-middle-class women, Marie made only the most minimal concessions to her pregnancy. In August, in her eighth month of pregnancy, she left Paris for the coastal town of Port-Blanc. Pierre was to join her later. In the meantime, the two exchanged frequent letters. Marie and Pierre spent so little time apart that these early letters are among the only records of their intimate relationship. Pierre, who was studying Marie's devilishly difficult native tongue, wrote in earnest, childish Polish: 'My little girl, so dear, so sweet, whom I love so much, I had your letter to-day and was very happy . . . Nothing new here, except that I miss you very much: my soul flew away with you.'[31] Marie's response is written in the simple Polish that Pierre could grasp. *I am very sad without you, come quickly, I expect you from morning to night and I don't see you coming . . . I am well, I work as much as I can, but Poincaré's book is more difficult than I had thought. I must speak to you about it and we can read over again together those parts which seemed to me important – and hard to understand.*[32]

Once Pierre made it to Port-Blanc, the couple set off, incredibly, on yet another bicycle romp, even though Marie was in the last month of pregnancy. Only after some days riding around the French countryside did Marie abandon the trip and return to Paris where she gave birth to a healthy daughter Irène on 12 September 1897. Marie noted the costs associated with the birth in her expenses book: *Champagne 3 fr. Telegrams 1 fr 10. Chemist and nurse: 71 fr. 50.* She wrote to her father of the details of caring for her infant daughter: *I am still nursing my little Queen, but lately we have been seriously afraid that I could not continue. For three weeks, the child's weight had suddenly gone down, Irène looked ill, and was depressed and lifeless. For some days now things have been going better. If the child gains weight normally I shall continue to nurse her. If not, I shall take a nurse, in spite of the grief this would be to me, and in spite of the expense; I don't want to interfere with my child's development for anything on earth. It is still very fine here, hot and sunny. Irène goes out with me for a walk every day, or else with the servant. I bathe her in a little washing basin.*[33] Marie had help with the baby from a nurse, and, more lastingly and tenderly, from Pierre's own father Eugène Curie, whose wife had died just days before Irène was born. Even with this help, Marie felt the burdens as well as the pleasures of caring for a newborn child, but they did not sway her in the least from her chosen path. Having secured the means to a salary with her *agrégation*, the next step was clear: a doctoral degree.

Discovering Radium · 1897–1902

Marie wanted to distinguish herself: she was less than eager to spend her life in the library, reading up on experiments others had performed. She was looking for fresh territory. Two momentous recent discoveries would guide her thinking. Just two years earlier Wilhelm Röntgen had discovered X-rays while playing with perhaps the most fertile scientific instrument of the 19th century: the cathode-ray tube. The cathode-ray tube (versions of which are still used today in most television sets and computer monitors) works by passing electrical currents through a vacuum created within a strong glass tube. The electric current generates glowing, phosphorescent light and as electrical and magnetic disturbances – then still imperfectly understood, and named cathode rays because they emanated from the cathode, or negatively charged electrode, in the tube. These new phenomena all demanded new theories to explain them. The excitement surrounding this apparatus meant that much undirected research was performed on cathode-ray tubes in the hopes of turning up clues to a deeper understanding of the relationship between electricity, magnetism, and matter.

It was serendipity – and an alert mind – that led Wilhelm Röntgen to the X-ray. He had been exploring the nature of the cathode rays that escaped from the vacuum tube in which they were produced. On 8 November 1895 Röntgen encased his vacuum tube in black cardboard, darkened his laboratory and turned on the current. Out of the corner of his eye he noticed a new glow in

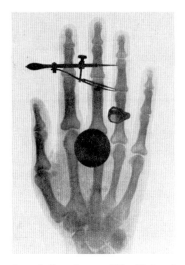

An early X-ray image of Mrs Röntgen's hand

The discoverer of X-rays, Wilhelm Röntgen

the laboratory, some distance away from his cathode ray tube. Turning off the current caused it to disappear. Upon further investigation it became clear that, though the vacuum tube was wrapped in cardboard so that no light could escape from it, some other kind of mysterious ray was emanating from the tube and causing a nearby barium platinocyanide-coated screen to fluoresce.

Further experiments revealed that the rays penetrated paper and copper but were blocked by human bones and certain metals. After some feverish weeks in the laboratory verifying his results, Röntgen published his discovery on 28 November 1895. In his paper, 'On a New Kind of Ray', he named the penetrating beams 'X-rays' because their exact nature eluded him. By January 1896 X-rays were front-page news and by February American newspaper publisher William Randolph Hearst was wiring Thomas Alva Edison to ask him to make a 'cathodograph' of the human brain. (He was unsuccessful.) An admiring public embraced X-rays from the start. The new rays were soon being put to a great variety

Ernest Rutherford, the New Zealand-born physicist who would later put forward the planetary model of the atom, began to experiment with X-rays shortly after Röntgen had discovered them. In a letter to his mother written in July 1896, Rutherford explains in a layperson's terms how X-rays are produced: 'The method is very simple. A little bulb is exhausted of air and an electrical discharge sent through. The bulb then lights up and looks of a greenish colour. The X-rays are given off and if a piece of cardboard with a certain chemical on it is held near it, metal objects placed behind can be seen through several inches of wood. The bones of the hand can be clearly seen and if one looks at a spectacle box, no trace of the wood is seen but only the metal rim and the glass. Aluminium allows the rays to go through easily . . . I see by the papers the other day that a blind person or persons without any eyeball [lens] can see them when the rays fall on the retina.'[34]

of practical uses, from the still-familiar medical task of diagnosing broken bones to now-forgotten applications in dermatology and hair-removal. From the first published image of Mrs Röntgen's hand to the countless displays of bullets embedded in shins, coins revealed in stomachs, and toes in ill-fitting shoes, X-rays grabbed the public's eye.

Röntgen's discovery and its widespread application focused interest on energetic rays of all kinds. Henri Becquerel, a professor of physics at the prestigious science university in Paris, the *École polytechnique* (Polytechnic college), was not immune to the wonder of X-rays. He decided to seek out natural sources of phosphorescence equivalent to those produced artificially in the cathode-ray tubes. Was there anything in nature with the same strange power to emit light without heat, penetrate solid matter, and leave an image on photographic plates? Becquerel started by examining certain substances that were known to emit light after being stimulated by sunlight. Might they also emit Röntgen's invisible X-rays? To test his theory, Becquerel wrapped photographic plates in lightproof black paper. He then placed a phosphorescent material on top of these plates – in this case uranium salts – and laid the experiment in the sun. If the sunlight caused the salts to give out visible light, perhaps the energy from the sun would also cause the salts to emit X-rays. Those rays should penetrate the black paper and the plates should show the outline of the uranium salts when developed.

Becquerel's initial results were positive: the outline of the uranium salts was clearly visible on the developed plates. Excitedly, he prepared a second experiment to corroborate his findings, but the Paris winter weather was uncooperative. He set the prepared experiment aside to wait for a sunny day, but after several days had passed, he decided to develop the plates anyway, despite not having exposed the salts to any sunlight. To his amazement the plates clearly showed the outline of the uranium salts. This must be, he surmised, a kind of 'invisible phosphorescence' coming from the salts themselves. But what exactly was the nature of this effect, seemingly related to Röntgen's X-rays, but produced without electricity or intervention of any sort?

Becquerel presented his results the very next evening to the Academy of Sciences, the august body that served as the voice of authority in French science, and his results were made public shortly thereafter. But while X-rays had received immediate and sustained attention from the public and the medical and scientific establishment, Becquerel's mysterious 'invisible phosphorescence' caused less of a stir. Perhaps the vivid, photographic impact of X-rays contributed to their imaginative power. 'Invisible phosphorescence' produced diffuse, fuzzy images, which did not reproduce

Henri Becquerel

particularly well and did not so inflame the imagination.

But Marie thought she had glimpsed something promising in the work of Becquerel, which others had left relatively unexamined. Becquerel's findings were curious. They were not easily explained according to the theories of cathode-ray tubes. The effects recorded were weaker than X-rays, though they seemed to be more sustained. Where was the energy coming from?

Curie began her research by begging various samples of metals, metallic compounds, and other minerals off colleagues at the EPCI and farther afield. At the start she wasn't too concerned what samples she obtained. She simply wanted to test as many as possible and so she cast a wide net. She began to test them in a disused machine shop made available to her by Pierre's sympathetic boss at the EPCI, Paul Schützenberger. Marie was grateful for the space, but the shed was damp and dusty (no mere inconvenience but a real challenge to the precise measurements she planned to make) and when she noted the icy temperature in the shed, one February morning, of 6.25 Celsius, she added ten exclamation marks in her otherwise inexpressive notebook. Once she had obtained her materials, found some coal to heat the small stove, and set up her instrumentation, Curie began to test her samples.

What exactly was she testing for? Instead of using photographic plates to measure their intensity, Curie focused on a peculiar feature of the rays that Becquerel had described. One of the many strange and interesting qualities of both X-rays and the spontaneously produced 'invisible phosphorescence' Curie studied was their ability to make the air around them conduct electricity. This effect had been described earlier in the year by the 73-year-old Lord Kelvin, who had applied his legendary skills in precision measurement to determine the degree to which such rays 'electrified' the air. This 'electrification' of the air offered the potential for extremely precise measurements and Marie Curie believed that precision was the way forward in research. Far from constituting a mere adjunct to creative discovery, she firmly thought that the development of better tools and techniques for measuring the properties of radiation would lead the way to further discoveries.

She decided to exploit this 'electrifying' property in her quest to find more such electrifying substances like the uranium salts Becquerel had used in his original experiment. Since little was known about these substances (and the samples Curie could procure were often small), she needed a precise and sensitive method for measuring exactly how much, if at all, a given substance was able to electrify the air around it. The instrument she chose was the piezoelectric quartz electrometer, the device invented by her husband and his brother. It could measure electrical current much more precisely than other instruments; in fact it offered a degree of precision for which there was no use until Marie Curie began her experiments. Curie used the device to test her samples. The crux of her rather intricate set-up was a kind of 'balance' that used the changing shape of the piezoelectric quartz crystal to translate the electrifying effect, if any, of each given sample into actual physical force. What had remained 'invisible phosphorescence' for Becquerel, Curie had managed to transform into a force she could literally feel with her hand.

Years later, a young colleague of Curie's would describe her mentor's admirable skill with her apparatus. 'She sat before the apparatus, making measurements in the half-darkness of an unheated room to avoid variations in temperature. The series of operations involved in opening the apparatus, pushing down the chronometer, lifting the weight, etc. as the piezoelectric method requires, is accomplished by Madame Curie with a discipline and perfect harmony of movements. No pianist could accomplish with greater virtuosity what the hands of Madame Curie accomplish in this special kind of work. It is a perfect technique which tends to reduce the coefficient of personal error to zero.'[35]

Most substances on the planet will cause no change in such an apparatus. But Curie was lucky and seemed to have an intuitive awareness of which elements might yield results. She did not have to wait long – just a few weeks – to see the instrument's needle shift, indicating the presence of the mysterious rays. The first results showed that thorium and its compounds exhibited the same phenomena as Becquerel had described. As it happened, Curie had unknowingly replicated the work of German scientist Gerhard Carl Schmidt, who had published his results a month earlier in Germany. Despite being scooped in this first discovery, her success was significant, and gave Curie a taste of the excitement that pushed her forward again and again. This thing in nature, whatever it was, that could expose photographic plates sealed in paper without energy from electricity or from the sun, was not an isolated element. There was a more general phenomenon at work. Her appetite whetted, she continued testing any materials she could get her hands on, this time focusing on establishing the intensity of the rays emitted by various compounds of uranium and thorium. She discovered that the mineral pitchblende, which contained uranium alongside many other elements, evinced a remarkably strong ability to render the air around it conductive, stronger indeed than a pure form of uranium did. On this basis, she deduced the presence of an element with much stronger properties than uranium itself. Her Sorbonne teacher Gabriel Lippmann announced the results for 'Marie Skłodowska Curie' at a meeting of the Academy of Sciences held on 12 April 1898. Marie had staked her claim.

At this point, Pierre's handwriting appears in the laboratory notebook that Marie had started alone. Marie's results were fascinating and potentially important; Pierre wanted to be a part of the ongoing research. He set aside his work on magnetism to help Marie prepare and test materials. Once Marie had embarked upon her investigative work and had developed the crucial instrumental set-up that allowed her to examine many different materials in a controlled and rapid manner, it was only a matter of time before she and Pierre stumbled on every chemist's dream: the discovery of a new element. Though it was not yet certified as a new element, on 20 July 1898 she announced her discovery of a new substance more active than uranium. She took the opportunity to honour her homeland. She sent the results to her cousin Józef Boguski at the same time as they were presented to the Academy, so that the news of a probably new element discovered by a Polish scientist in France was published in Warsaw in a monthly photographic review called *Swiatlo* just as soon as it was in Paris. *If the existence of this new metal is confirmed*, wrote the Curies, *we propose to call it polonium, from the name of the original country of one of us.*[36]

Marie and Pierre's momentous discovery, which would lead to even greater findings, did not interrupt their normal routine. Marie continued to note Irène's growth in a school notebook covered in grey linen, where she had recorded her fluctuating weight, food preferences, and succession of 'firsts'. Just two days after the polonium announcement, she wrote *Irène says 'thanks' with her hand. She can walk very well now on all fours. She says 'Gogli, gogli, go.' She stays in the garden all day at Sceaux on a carpet. She can roll, pick herself up, and sit down.*[37]

It seems remarkable, but after the excitement of these early results, all obtained within three months, Marie and Pierre closed up their humble research space and took their annual summer holiday. They would not return to their path-breaking work for five months. They rented a peasant's house in Auvergne, where they had once spent the night cycling by moonlight, and took more bicycle rides, swam in rivers, and discussed the work they would resume on their return. This long break also helped them to recover from the stifling air at the laboratory on rue Lhomond, where, though they did not realize it, their exposure to radiation was giving them aches, pains, and fatigue.

On their return, Marie also had to cope with the departure of her sister Bronia. She and Kazimierz were moving to Austrian Poland to build a sanatorium for patients suffering from tuberculosis. Marie and Bronia were both deeply saddened to be separated. Shortly after her sister's departure, Marie wrote to Bronia about her sense of loss and asked for sisterly advice on child rearing: *You can't imagine what a void you have made in my life. I have lost everything I clung to in Paris except my husband and my child. It seems to me that Paris no longer exists, apart from our lodging and the school where we work . . . Irène is getting to be a big girl. She is very difficult about her food, and except milk tapioca she will eat hardly anything regularly, not even eggs. Write me what would be a suitable menu for persons of her age.*[38] In the midst of her sadness at losing her sister, the difficulties of raising a young child, and the excitement of her research, Marie Curie also found time to make a winter's supply of gooseberry jelly. Her notes in the margins of a cookbook entitled *Family Cooking* reveal the pleasure she took in precision and careful method at home: *I took eight pounds of fruit and the same weight in crystallized sugar. After boiling for ten minutes, I passed the mixture through a rather fine sieve. I obtained fourteen pots of very good jelly, not transparent, which 'took' perfectly.*[39]

In November the laboratory notebook begins again in earnest, and by December 1898 Marie and Pierre had identified the presence of another highly active substance in pitchblende. This time it was a substance that would make them famous. After confirming the existence of the new element through spectroscopy, a technique that allowed them to chemically 'fingerprint' the new element, the Curies published the results of their work in December along with their collaborator Gustave Bémont, the head chemist at the EPCI. They called the new substance radium, because of the powerful radiation it emitted. In a pair of papers announcing the results

Pierre (centre) and Marie, with Pierre's assistant Petit, in the laboratory where radium and polonium were discovered

to the Academy of Sciences, the Curies coined the term 'radioactive' to describe how strongly a given substance electrified the air around it. Polonium was 400 times more radioactive than uranium, the Curies reported, and radium was a remarkable 900 times more radioactive (eventually, they would show that it was one million times more active than uranium). While polonium had been frustratingly difficult to identify chemically (it is now understood to be an element that decays rapidly and so is difficult to work with in the laboratory), radium presented a unique line on the spectrographic record. (A spectrograph is an instrument capable of representing the chemical composition of a substance in graphic form.) The evidence strongly suggested that it was a new element.

'AN ATOMIC PROPERTY'

The discovery of a new element would be, for any chemist, a crowning achievement. But what Marie and Pierre had discovered immediately before and after their five-month holiday was more than

DISCOVERY OF RADIUM

just a new addition to the periodic table. Out of this early research, accomplished in a few months in 1898, came Marie Curie's most significant scientific observation. The insight was this: radioactivity is an atomic property of matter. Curie arrived at this conclusion from a straightforward appraisal of the facts, made possible by her precise measurement of samples using the Curie brothers' piezoelectric device. The activity of the uranium compounds she examined, such as pitchblende, depended solely on the amount of radioactive material present. While chemical reactions depend on variable external factors such as temperature or sunlight or the presence of other chemicals, Marie's radioactive substances emitted the same amount of energy no matter how she manipulated them. Hot or cold, solid or gaseous, in compound or pure, the quantity

The atom has an impressive pedigree, dating back to the ancient Greek philosopher Democritus, who coined the term (literally meaning 'indivisible') to describe the basic and immutable building blocks of matter. Isaac Newton (1642–1727) assumed a stable unit of matter when formulating his rules of force and motion, without explaining what such a unit might consist of. After Newton's death, 18th-century researchers tried to integrate Newtonian mechanics with their study of the 'imponderables' – phenomena such as electricity, magnetism, heat, and light. Through the 19th century, physicists and chemists developed increasingly complex models of atomic structure to reconcile the wave-like nature of light and heat with evidence that matter existed as discrete particles. At the time of Marie and Pierre Curie's discovery of

polonium and radium, there was no consensus on the nature, or even the existence, of the atom. Our modern 'planetary' model of the atom is a modified version of a model first proposed by Ernest Rutherford in 1911. Our current model of the atom (in simplified terms) contains three basic particles: the proton, the neutron, and the electron. The nucleus, or inner core of the atom, consists of heavy, positively charged protons together with slightly heavier, chargeless neutrons. Negatively charged, nearly massless electrons circle the nucleus in various orbits. The number of protons in an element is constant and determines its atomic number. The same element may contain different numbers of neutrons, however: these chemically similar forms of an element are called isotopes.

of radioactive element alone determined the degree to which a compound 'electrified' the air around it. From this observation, firmly grounded in her systematic investigations in the laboratory and dependent almost solely on the traditional tools of chemistry, Curie arrived at her insight that the phenomenon she named radioactivity was linked in some fundamental way to the atomic structure of the element.

In her biography of Pierre, Curie later wrote: *My experiments proved that the radiation of uranium compounds . . . is an atomic property of the element of uranium. Its intensity is proportional to the quantity of uranium contained in the compound, and depends neither on conditions of chemical combination, nor on external circumstances, such as light and temperature.*[40] Marie and Pierre were witnessing a completely new phenomenon – and it looked like a kind of natural perpetual energy machine. This phenomenon would later prove profoundly important to the field that would become nuclear physics, hinting that there was an interior instability to the once immutable atom and a source of energy far greater than the largest coal mine or electrical dynamo could provide.

In stating that the strange phenomenon of radioactivity was rooted within the atom, Marie Curie began a theoretical upheaval that would replace a vision of the universe as a stable theatre for the Newtonian mechanics of force and motion with an uncertain, unstable quantum universe. In 1898 the prevailing vision of the fundamental units of matter as a version of Isaac Newton's billiard ball atoms – 'solid, massy, hard, impenetrable particles' – had just begun to crack. In 1897 J J Thomson, head of the Cavendish Laboratory at Cambridge University, had discovered the electron, the first subatomic particle. He did so by experimenting with the same sorts of cathode rays that had led Röntgen to his discovery of X-rays just a few years earlier. Thomson's students playfully sent up their teacher's discovery in a ditty:

THE ATOM UNDER ATTACK

All preconceived notions he sets at defiance
By means of some neat and ingenious appliance
By which he discovers some new law of science
Which no one had ever suspected before.
All the chemists went off into fits;
Some of them thought they were losing their wits,
When quite without warning
(Their theories scorning)
The atom one morning
He broke into bits[41]

At the Cavendish at least, as this light-hearted song reveals, atoms, and unstable atoms at that, were considered real if still somewhat sensational. But such broken atoms threatened the 'preconceived notions' held by the public and the scientific community alike. Despite the cheery confidence of the Cavendish ditty, elsewhere the controversy over the nature of matter still raged. Proponents of the aether theory believed in a solid yet imperceptible medium through which electricity, magnetism, and gravity traveled. They had no need for atomic or subatomic particles to account for the phenomena generated by the cathode-ray tube. Even the very existence of atoms was disputed by well-regarded physicists such as Ernst Mach, who believed them to be no more than a theoretical crutch, a model for describing certain phenomena that in fact bore little resemblance to the way things actually were. For most of those who did believe in the existence of a fundamental unit of matter, that unit was necessarily stable. Any changes in structure at the atomic level were considered the shady business of alchemy – changing ordinary metals into gold – not proper science. Good scientists did not think of perverting nature in such a way, if they thought it was possible at all.

Marie Curie led the way to the unstable atom and thus helped open the door to the great and terrifying discoveries of atomic energy made in the 20th century. Her clarity of vision and her ability to control for variation while measuring with a precise and steady hand allowed her to distinguish the essential characteristic of a very strange sort of element. In a few months of feverish work in 1898 she made a discovery that would support a lifetime of research. Marie Curie never again made as profound a statement or as inspired an intuitive leap as she did in suggesting that the atoms of this new element radium were themselves somehow responsible for the radioactivity she was measuring. Her early work had straddled the gulf between chemistry and physics. From now on Marie would remain focused on the task of identifying those elements responsible for this atomic radiation. In the future, it would be Pierre, by now completely committed to the elements that he and Marie had discovered together, who would take on the role of physicist investigating the nature of the novel phenomenon.

Marie continued to work on perfecting the special chemical tools needed to tease this strange new beast from the black rock in which it was found. Her stated reason for isolating pure radium was to prove its existence to the scientific community. *In our opinion,* she wrote in her biography of Pierre, *there could be no doubt of the existence of the new elements, but to make chemists admit their existence, it was necessary to isolate them.*[42] But for many chemists as well as physicists, the evidence her early research had garnered was sufficient to ensure radium's standing as a bona fide element. There was something else driving Curie's desire to isolate radium. Curie's steadfast belief in the importance of accumulating radium, indeed her vision of accumulation as a scientific activity in itself, would shape the rest of her career. In a way, the isolation of radium, which would take three years and continue, in one way or another, to occupy her long afterwards, was less the necessary proof required by a faceless scientific community (as Curie saw it), than the logical continuation

Radiation is a general term for any energy travelling in a wave form, including heat, light, X-rays, and infrared beams. But the word is often used as shorthand for the more precise term 'ionizing radiation', a biologically damaging form of energy produced by atoms of certain substances as they change from unstable to stable forms. Substances that naturally emit such radiation – such as uranium or radium – are said to be radioactive; the process by which their atoms give off radiation is called decay. Ionizing radiation comes in two forms: electromagnetic radiation and particle radiation. X-rays and gamma rays are part of the same spectrum of electromagnetic energy that also includes ultraviolet light, visible light, infrared, and radio waves. These massless and chargeless rays are produced by the nuclei of atoms under-going nuclear decay; they are also produced by the sun, and exist as part of the background of cosmic radiation left over from the Big Bang. Because they have no mass, these rays are highly penetrating; gamma and X-rays require several feet of concrete to block them. Decaying nuclei also release ionizing radiation in the form of high-energy particles, streams of which make up particle radiation, such as alpha and beta rays. Formed of two protons and two neutrons, alpha particles are positively charged, large, heavy, and slow-travelling. Because they are so big, they can be blocked by human skin or a sheet of paper. Beta particles are smaller, negatively-charged electrons emitted by the nucleus; they pass through paper and wood but are stopped by lead.

of a methodical and painstaking manner of working and understanding that had already stood her in such good stead.

'THIS MISERABLE OLD SHED'

Once again, Curie set about securing raw materials from which to isolate radium and polonium and a laboratory in which to do it. Once again, Paul Schützenberger, the director at the EPCI, provided a space for her, in yet another abandoned shed (the school seems to have been rich in them), which had once been used as a dissecting room of the School of Medicine. These conditions, hardly ideal, have become part of the Curie legend. *Its glass roof did not afford complete shelter against rain; the heat was suffocating in summer, and the bitter cold of winter was only a little lessened by the iron stove.*[43] Despite the rude surroundings, described by one visiting chemist as a 'cross between a stable and a potato-cellar',[44] it was, in Marie Curie's own words, *in this miserable old shed that we passed the best and happiest years of our life, devoting our entire days to our work*.[45] The rough conditions seem to have suited Curie's sense of her suffering as a mark of her lofty disregard for material gain. *It was like creating something out of nothing, and if my earlier studying years had once been called by my brother-in-law the heroic period of my life, I can say without exaggeration that the period in which my husband and I now entered was truly the heroic one of our common life.*[46]

The 'miserable old shed' where Curie worked

The challenges of securing adequate laboratory space, though extreme for Marie and Pierre Curie, were far from unusual for scientists in late 19th-century France. While 'modern' science was often held up as an ideal of the new French Republic, the state's coffers creaked open reluctantly. When funds were made available, they were most likely to be in the form of a prize that rewarded research already accomplished than a grant that encouraged future work. In 1900, nine times as much money was dispensed in the form of prizes than as grant money in France. In Germany and England this ratio was nearly reversed.[47]

On top of the general disorganization in science funding at this time, Pierre and Marie Curie were both further disadvantaged. In 1899, Marie Curie was a 32-year-old woman with no doctoral degree and no official relationship with a research establishment. At 40, Pierre had spent his adult life avoiding the formal institutions of French science. He was notoriously averse to what he saw as hasty publishing and meaningless networking, and would not patent his inventions and discoveries, despite the research he could

The laboratory as we know it is a 19th-century invention. Before 1855, there were no spaces in British universities dedicated to the study and teaching of the experimental sciences. Chemistry was pursued in basement rooms closer in spirit to the kitchen than the modern lab. And physics was the avocation of wealthy gentlemen such as William Thomson (later Lord Kelvin) and Henry Cavendish who could afford to build private laboratories in their homes. By 1875, 25 new physics laboratories had been built in Britain. Parallel developments in Germany and, to a lesser extent, France generated an international community of professional physicists for the first time. Laboratories were, from the start, spaces for teaching as well as research. Senior scientists trained students in the new skills of precision measurement and hands-on experimentation that were increasingly in demand, particularly in the fast-growing telegraphy industry. New provisions for mandatory education also created a need for secondary school teachers trained in the mathematical sciences, which were increasingly seen as critical to national identity and self-sufficiency.

have undertaken with any revenues he might have gained from doing so.

It is fair to say that Curie embarked on her 'fruitful years', as her daughter Eve later called them, without knowing exactly what she was getting into. From her earlier studies she knew that the quantities of radium and polonium contained in the mineral pitchblende were small, perhaps as little as 1 per cent. As she began to purify the element more thoroughly, it became apparent that *the new radioactive element could exist only in quite minute proportion.*[48] Only trace quantities of the elements radium and polonium were present in the pitchblende, meaning both that its radioactive properties must be even stronger than expected and that much more work would be required to isolate even one thousandth of a gram of the material. *Would we have insisted, despite the scarcity of our means of research, if we had known the true proportion of what we were searching for, no one can tell; all that can be said now is that the constant progress of our work held us absorbed in a passionate research.*[49]

While they worked, Marie and Pierre speculated on the nature of the element they sought in the dark and lustrous pitchblende.

Their daughter Eve re-created their thoughts as the musings of expectant parents. '"I wonder what *It* will be like, what *It* will look like," Marie said one day with the feverish curiosity of a child who has been promised a toy. "Pierre, what form do you imagine *It* will take?" "I don't know," the physicist answered gently. "I should like it to have a very beautiful colour . . . "'[50]

Marie Curie, faced with a new notoriety, began to paint herself and her work in only the driest of terms. Rather than revealing the wonder she felt in the face of her discovery, Marie resorted to what she saw as the correct style for scientific communication: devoid of emotion and personality. This tactic must have seemed wise to Marie, as a woman working in a brand new field. But it has meant that her own voice, the distinctive and private voice that might reveal the motivations and responses of the person behind the scientific triumphs, is very faint. Even in a letter to her sister written in 1899, Marie is matter-of-fact about work which was, at that point, the most exciting she had ever undertaken: *Our life is always the same. We work a lot but we sleep well, so our health does not suffer. The evenings are taken up by caring for the child. In the morning I dress her and give her her food, then I can generally go out at about nine. During the whole of this year we have not been either to the theatre or a concert, and we have not paid one visit . . . I miss my family enormously, above all you, my dears, and Father. I often think of my isolation with grief. I cannot complain of anything else, for our health is not bad, the child is growing well, and I have the best husband one could dream of; I could never have imagined finding one like him. He is a true gift of heaven, and the more we live together the more we love each other. Our work is progressing.*[51] Her deep love for her husband is apparent, but Curie's letter otherwise gives no hint of the exciting developments in her working life. Aside from the letters reproduced in her daughter's biography (the originals were destroyed during bombing in Warsaw in World War Two) and a very few autobiographical accounts, there is scant evidence of what the 32-year-old really thought as she was doing the work which would earn her two Nobel Prizes.

From the point of view of scientific publications, this was the most productive period of the Curies' lives. In 1900 alone, Pierre published five papers and Marie published three. Together they reported 'On the Atomic Weight of Radiferous Barium', and, more generally on 'The New Radioactive Substances and the Rays They Emit'. Pierre went on to publish ten more papers in the following two years, based on his theoretical work on radioactivity, including a paper with Henri Becquerel on the effect of radium rays on living organisms and one on induced radioactivity provoked by radium salts. Marie, perhaps more occupied with the daily activity of the purification process, not to mention the demands of running a household and caring for a two-year-old, published just one more paper in that time.

'HALF-SCIENTIFIC, HALF-INDUSTRIAL'

Curie had carried out her initial investigations on apple-sized chunks of minerals on a table top in a disused machine shop. But once she decided to pursue the isolation of more than a trace quantity of pure radium, the scale of her operation changed rapidly. When it became apparent that not kilograms but tonnes of material would be needed, Curie, the would-be recluse, demonstrated her skill in negotiating with both academic and industrial sources. Nearly from the moment she decided to isolate a quantity of radium, the Curie laboratory was a semi-industrial affair. Though it has often been told as a story of one woman (or one couple) struggling alone in an ill-equipped laboratory, Marie Curie always knew that the isolation of radium would need to be a collaborative venture. *Our work on radioactivity began in solitude,* she recounted. *But before the breadth of this task it became more and more evident that collaboration would be useful.*[52] At the time, pitchblende was notable only as a by-product of uranium mining, mined almost exclusively from the St Joachimsthal mine in what was then the Austro-Hungarian Empire, today the Czech Republic. Once the uranium (mined for use as a yellow glass dye) had been removed from the glossy black pitchblende, the rest was waste as far as the mine was concerned. This residue was exactly what Marie and Pierre needed. This suited both sides perfectly: the mine cleared out unwanted material and the Curies received pitchblende that had been already relieved of the bulk of its uranium, a relatively weakly radioactive element in which they were not interested. Once they had ascertained that the pitchblende was of adequate quality, Marie and Pierre negotiated with the Austrian government to secure the substantial amounts of the mineral they needed for their great project.

In early 1899, tonnes of pitchblende in burlap sacks arrived at the EPCI. The heavy sacks were filled with black powdered pitchblende mixed with pine needles from the Austrian forest where it had been excavated. Over the next three years, Marie and Pierre, working together in the glassed-in shed, would whittle the tonnes of pitchblende down to one tenth of a gram of pure radium.

This accomplishment has become a touchstone of the Curie story. The classic image of Curie is of her toiling over the furnace in her humble shed, boiling pots of pitchblende down like gooseberry jam. It is this stubborn persistence, bordering on obsession, that has endured as the kernel of the Curie myth. At the beginning Marie's intense drive to purify radium was born of a chemist's desire to handle the element in quantities that were suitable for chemical analysis. In later years, her accumulation of pure radium would become the foundation of her political and scientific influence.

First, the radium needed to be separated from the tonnes of pitchblende in which it lurked. Partly for efficiency's sake and partly, one senses, because it suited their respective tastes, Marie and Pierre divided up the task. Pierre continued the investigations into the physical properties of radium on which they had already published several papers while Marie assumed responsibility for the chemical experiments necessary to produce pure radium.

This division of labour, and her devotion to the task, all too easily grew into the myth of Curie as a saintly chemist drudge, taking care of the chemical 'busy work' by purifying radium 'by painstaking, wet chemical methods from millions of grams of crude starting material', in the shadow of her physicist husband Pierre's deeper theoretical understanding.[53] A 1904 *Vanity Fair* caricature of the then-famous couple shows Marie standing behind Pierre, gripping his arm and the table, as if for support. A medley of test tubes and vials crowds the table. Pierre stands, trim and natty in a double-breasted suit, holding up a tube of glowing radium, his other hand marking his place in a half-finished book. Marie may be his accomplice, caught up in the discovery, but the implication that Pierre is leading the way is clear. The real picture is of course more complex. It is true that during her working life Curie devoted vastly more time and energy to solving puzzles of chemistry and the elucidation of the periodic table of elements than she did to grappling with a theory that might account for the behaviour of the elements she worked so hard to isolate and define. But her qualifications as a mathematician and physicist as well as chemist were formidable, and, by formal standards, stronger than those of her husband. Often he turned to her for help with a difficult problem in mathematics

A 1904 *Vanity Fair* caricature

or to ask her opinion on a possible mechanism for radioactivity.

The myth has this much truth: the isolation of radium, though tedious and highly labour-intensive, was a relatively mechanical and certain process – given enough raw material to work with. The chemical separation and purification of 'glow-worm' radium from pitchblende required no more than a clever application of the traditional tools of physical chemistry, a subtle and expert sifting of materials. By repeatedly boiling the material, crystallizing it, and then separating those samples into 'fractions' that contained the radioactive portion in slightly greater proportion, Curie was slowly able to separate the radioactive substance from the other elements present in the pitchblende.

Although it did not differ greatly from traditional practices in chemistry, Curie's own descriptions of the process reveal it to be physically demanding work. *I had to work with as much as twenty kilograms of material at a time, so that the hangar was filled with great vessels full of precipitates and of liquids. It was exhausting work to move the containers about, to transfer the liquids, and to stir for hours at a time, with an iron bar, the boiling material in the cast iron basins. I extracted from the mineral the radium-bearing barium and this, in the state of chloride, I submitted to a fractional crystallization.*[54]

As they worked, Marie and Pierre slowly witnessed something wondrous. Just as Pierre had hoped, radium did have a special colour. It glowed in the dark, an eerie blue-green which intensified as it became more pure. *We had an especial joy, Marie remembered, in observing that our products containing concentrated radium were all spontaneously luminous. My husband who hoped to see them show beautiful colourations had to agree that this other unhoped-for characteristic gave him even greater satisfaction . . . [these products] were arranged on tables and boards [in the laboratory]; from all sides we could see their slightly luminous silhouettes, and these gleamings, which seemed suspended in the darkness, stirred us with ever new emotion and enchantment.*[55]

In addition to creating its own light, radium also made other substances, such as diamonds, phosphorescent, allowing fakes to be easily determined. One other property of radium was as troubling as it was intriguing: its radiation was 'contagious', rendering objects it came near to radioactive. *When one studies strongly radioactive substances,* Marie advised, *special precautions must be taken if one wishes to be able to continue taking delicate measurements. The various objects used in a chemical laboratory, and those which serve for experiments in physics, all become radioactive in a short time and act upon photographic plates through black paper. Dust, the air of the room, and one's clothes all become radioactive. The air in the room is a conductor. In the laboratory where we work the evil has reached an acute stage, and we can no longer have any apparatus completely isolated.*[56] From the very beginning, Marie's joy in the special qualities of the substance she had discovered was tempered by an awareness that its properties could be troublesome and difficult to control. But while she understood, and measured, the extent of the radioactive contamination, she made no attempt to limit her own exposure to radium, or that of other workers.

Marie sought ever better ways of purifying as much radium as possible. Almost immediately following their announcement of the discovery of radium in 1899, the Curies approached the scientific instrument-maker *Société Centrale des Produits Chimiques* (Central Chemical Products Company) to help them develop a semi-industrial method of processing pitchblende.[57] This company had already produced and sold scientific instruments designed by Pierre Curie. Together, the Curies and the *Société Centrale* developed a unique collaborative process for isolating radium. The heaviest work was done in the factory, where large vats of minerals were ground, heated, boiled, and separated. Once the physical separation had progressed as far as it could without scientific expertise, the products were taken to the Curies' laboratory. There, Marie Curie used her piezoelectric technique to measure the amount of radioactive material in a given sample. By alternating these measurements with the continual purification and fractionization of the material, she was able to slowly isolate the radioactive parts of the mineral into one small sample. It was like sifting through a mountain of sand to find one grain, similar to the others in most respects save one, its radioactive beacon, which Curie was able to detect with the piezoelectric device.

Headed by André Debierne, a former student of Pierre Curie and assistant at the Faculty of Sciences, the *Société Centrale* project lasted for four years, until the end of 1903. The *Société*'s reward came in the form of radium salts that it could then market in the burgeoning radium industry. The Curie laboratory gained cheap access to chemicals and staff paid for by the *Société*, as well as receiving their share of the radium extract. After this early partnership Marie Curie continued throughout her life to seek technical and financial help from business and industry. She collaborated with the industrial chemist, Armet de Lisle, who created a radium factory outside Paris at Nogent-sur-Marne after 1904. Curie would work closely with Armet de Lisle until his death in 1928, commissioning the treatment of tonnes of pitchblende and lending technical advice on the development of chemical processes. Relations between the Armet de Lisle factory and the Curie laboratory were close. Jacques Danne, a former assistant to Pierre Curie, oversaw the factory for Armet de Lisle and helped to edit the new journal published by de Lisle, *Le Radium*.

Le Radium effectively served as the house publication of the Curie laboratory, through which the new work with radium could be communicated to a diverse audience. The front cover photographs from its first two issues show clearly that radium work was both scientific and industrial. On the front cover of the first issue, published in January 1904, is a picture of Pierre, Marie, and Pierre's assistant Petit, in the laboratory on rue Lhomond. Marie Curie wears a loose white blouse and her hair is in a bun. She sits in front of a piezoelectric device measuring a sample. Her eyes are focused on the instrument dial; her hands carefully manipulate the device. Pierre and Petit stare intently at the camera. They wear suits with white collars and ties. It is a scene of quiet meditation and precise measurement – a laboratory. By contrast, the front cover of the second issue depicts a factory scene: two men in work clothes toiling at vats of boiling material set over rough brick ovens.

Le Radium presented radioactivity as an international and inter-disciplinary field that encompassed both theoretical and experimental physics, as well as precision measurement and chemical analysis. Articles on physics, chemistry, measurement, and geology share space with advertisements for electroscopes, wireless telegraphy equipment, and instruments for storing radium. The work of Marie Curie received pride of place on the front page and pieces by workers in her laboratory were designated as such. Many, but by no means all, of the articles originated in the Curie laboratory. The journal contained original contributions by Hans Geiger, who

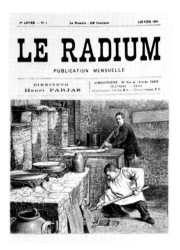

The first two issues of *Le Radium*, 1904

later invented of the device used to measure radioactivity that bears his name, Frederick Soddy, Rutherford's collaborator in developing the theory of atomic transmutation, physicist Paul Langevin, and Robert Millikan, the American experimentalist who was the first to measure the charge of a single electron.

As her place in this international journal makes clear, Marie Curie's world extended far beyond the walls of the laboratory on rue Lhomond. After the initial alliances with the *Société Centrale des Produits Chimiques* and the factory of Armet de Lisle, the laboratory had contact over the years with many other chemical and mining companies such as *Minerals & Métaux* (Minerals and Metals) the *Société Française d'Énergie et de Radio-Chimie* (The French Energy and Radio-Chemistry Company) and the *Société Minière Industrielle Franco-Brésilienne* (The Franco-Brazilian Industrial Mining Company) which supplied the raw materials needed. Later, Curie began a close collaboration with a mining company in the Belgian Congo – where there were large uranium reserves – which began in 1924 and lasted until her death. The company benefited from Curie's expertise in methods of extraction; Curie benefited from ever more radioactive material to study. In all her dealings with business, Curie's practical knowledge of how best to extract radium from pitchblende was her greatest asset. Over the course of a lifetime she used her knowledge – and the power that came with it – to amass a fortune in radium and build a solid foundation for the study of radioactivity in France.

From the first announcement of their discovery, Marie and Pierre Curie were famous. Journalists delighted in the picturesque shed, the quiet romance, and the shared ideals of the sombre scientists. Marie was routinely portrayed as a kind of saint. The image of her with a halo of backlit hair, examining what the viewer is encouraged to believe are the precious contents of a rather small test tube, is only the most explicit of these renderings. In none of her numerous portraits is she smiling.

The son of a Scottish wheelwright and an English schoolteacher, Ernest Rutherford was born in Nelson, New Zealand, on 30 August 1871. In 1894, after successful undergraduate study in New Zealand, he received an 1851 Exhibition Science Scholarship enabling him to go to Trinity College, Cambridge, as a research student at the Cavendish Laboratory under J J Thomson. A gifted experimenter as well as a bold theoretician, the brash Rutherford was quickly recognized as an exceptional student. While at the Cavendish, he invented a detector for electromagnetic waves and reported the existence of alpha and beta rays in uranium radiation. In 1898, he became professor of physics at McGill University, Montreal, continuing his work on alpha rays and developing the theory of radioactive decay with Frederick Soddy. By 1907, he was back in England, first as a professor at Manchester University where, with Hans Geiger, he worked on the detection of a single alpha particle and a method to count the particles emitted by radium. In 1908, he received the Nobel Prize in chemistry for his research on the disintegration of elements and the chemistry of radioactive substances. In 1919, he became the head of the Cavendish Laboratory, directing the research of many future Nobel laureates. Rutherford was knighted in 1914, appointed to the Order of Merit in 1925, and in 1931 he was created First Baron Rutherford of Nelson, New Zealand, and Cambridge. He died on 19 October 1937 and was buried in Westminster Abbey, near the tombs of Isaac Newton and Lord Kelvin.

Scientists abroad had taken notice of the Curies' successes and were working hard to uncover the secrets of the glowing radium. Foremost among them was the physicist Ernest Rutherford. He was then living in Cambridge, working at the famous Cavendish Laboratory under J J Thomson. In a letter to his mother, he wrote, 'I have to keep going as there are always people on my track. I have to publish my present as rapidly as possible in order to keep in the race. The best sprinters in this road of investigation are Becquerel and the Curies in Paris who have done a great deal of very important work in the subject of radioactive bodies during the last few years.'[58]

As far as Rutherford was concerned, the race was on.

Theorizing Radioactivity · 1902–1906

Marie Curie had in fact little interest in the race to theorize the inner workings of radium. Ernest Rutherford himself commented in 1903 that 'M and Mme Curie have throughout taken a very general view of the phenomena of radioactivity, and have not put forward any definite theory.'[59] Rutherford did not mean this as a compliment, though the Curies may have considered it one; their hearts did not lie in the theoretical universe.

In their 1902 manifesto 'On radioactive substances', the Curies speculated briefly on the nature of the energy which they had observed. *If we seek to fix the origin of the energy of radioactivity, we may make various assumptions, which group around two quite general hypotheses: (1) each radioactive atom possesses in the form of potential energy the energy it releases; (2) the radioactive atom is a mechanism which at each instant draws in from outside itself the energy it releases.*[60] The first hypothesis, which time has shown to be the correct one, offered a then seemingly intractable puzzle to the Curies.

If each atom constantly releases energy from an internal store without drawing on external sources to replenish itself, shouldn't the atom be in some way altered? Yet experiments done at the time failed to identify any change in the weight or spectrum of radium-bearing substances. This would have made radioactivity an eternal source of energy, in defiance of the surest truth of 19th-century physics and chemistry, the conservation of energy. (The law of the conservation of energy states that energy can never be created or destroyed, only converted from one form into another, such as the conversion of electricity into heat and light in a light bulb.)

Given what seemed an impossible first hypothesis, the Curies turned to the second. The notion that radioactive substances were absorbing energy from outside sources was a more comfortable one, if no more certain. They suggested a few possibilities. The energy might be drawn as heat from the surrounding atmosphere or it might be absorbed from *other radiations unknown to us, since it is indeed probable that we know little about the medium that surrounds us, since our knowledge is limited to phenomena which can affect our senses directly or indirectly.*[61]

But having come so far in their theorizing on the possible mechanisms that might account for radium's strange properties, the Curies were reluctant to go further. No one was more aware than they of the strange, seemingly contradictory properties of radium. Radium produced heat like a chemical reaction but the nature of this heat-production was obviously not chemical. If the heat was produced by some sort of transformation, that change must take place within the atom itself. And if this were so, the final conclusion was clear: *Consequently, from this point of view, the atom of radium would be in a process of evolution, and we should be forced to abandon the theory of the invariability of atoms, which is at the foundation of modern chemistry.*[62] Rather than attempting to generate a coherent theory that would account for the mysterious properties of radioactive matter, they merely re-asserted their central assumption that radioactivity was in some way essentially atomic and pointed the way to further experimentation. Given the atomic nature of radioactivity, they explained, *we can draw greatly varied consequences to be submitted to the control of experience without our having to specify precisely where the radioactive substance obtains that energy.*[63] Precision, the heart of the Curies' experimental practice, was curiously absent from their theorizing. *Precise hypotheses almost certainly contain a portion of error along with a portion of truth.*[64] If a vague theory could be some protection against a hasty error, the Curies were willing to settle for it.

Marie Curie's theoretical caution is perhaps linked to her background in the gradualist tradition of Polish positivism. But one also senses that Curie felt a real joy in developing her methods of precise measurement and experimentation. For Curie, it was the techniques she perfected with her boiling pots and delicate instrumentation that lit the way forward towards truth.

'THE PRIMARY FOUNTAINS OF ENERGY'

The Curies' hypothesis that the radium atom 'drew in' energy from outside itself was destined to be disproved. Ernest Rutherford and Frederick Soddy, working together at McGill University in Canada in the first years of the 20th century, took up the challenge of elaborating a full theory of atomic transmutation. Today their 1902 paper 'The Cause and Nature of Radioactivity' has a familiar ring to it: they talk about radiation more or less the way we still talk about it today. The Curies had been reluctant to contradict the law of conservation of energy. Rutherford and Soddy showed that radioactivity did not contradict the law of conservation of energy but bid the stable atom *adieu*: 'Radioactivity is shown to be accompanied by chemical changes in which new types of matter are being continuously produced.'[65] It was the Curies' observations of radium – and faith in the immutability of the atom – that had been misleading. Radium's atoms actually do decay, but so slowly – it has a half-life of 1,620 years – that the instruments available to Curie and the experiments she devised to measure the decay could not detect the change.

Rutherford recognized the need for a canny presentation of a controversial new theory of matter about which he himself had little doubt. 'Although of course it is not advisable to put the case too bluntly to a chemical society, I believe that in the radioactive elements we have a process of disintegration or transmutation

Ernest Rutherford

steadily going on which is the source of the energy dissipated in radioactivity.'[66] In the formal paper of 1902 with which they announced their theory, Rutherford and Soddy eschewed the term *transmutation* in favour of the less jolting *transformation*: 'The radioactive elements must be undergoing spontaneous transformation . . . It is apparent that we are dealing with phenomena outside the sphere of known atomic forces. Radioactivity may therefore be considered as a manifestation of subatomic chemical change.'[67]

Soddy realized that their new theory of radiation was like a modern version of the old alchemist's dream of turning base metals into gold. The transmutability of the elements in radioactivity heralded a new kind of gold: an awesome supply of energy. In his 1909 *Interpretation of Radium*, a popularized account of the discovery and properties of the new element, Soddy wrote that 'if it were possible artificially to disintegrate an element with a heavier atom than gold and produce gold from it so great an amount of energy would probably be evolved that the gold in comparison would be of little account. The energy would be far more valuable than the gold.'[68] He ended by saying, 'It was a legitimate aspiration to believe that one day [Man] would attain the power to regulate for his own purposes the primary fountains of energy which Nature now so jealously conserves for the future.'[69]

Words like these today conjure instantly not a fountain of energy but the mushroom cloud of the atomic bomb. But in Curie's time radium, far from being feared, was welcomed as a wonder element. Almost as soon as it was being prepared on an large scale, it was in great demand. Part of the demand was industrial: radium was used to paint glow-in-the-dark instrument and watch dials. But the uses of radium that most thoroughly captured the public's imagination were medical and cosmetic. Because radium was known to kill certain diseased tissues, and to 'burn' the skin in a way that seemed to cure some dermatological conditions, the luminous element became a cross between a wonder drug and a fountain of youth, a cancer-cure-cum-cellulite-cream. Potions of every variety were sold under mostly spurious claims promising the blemish-free skin of youth.

'Radioactivity is an essential element for maintaining healthy skin cells', crooned one advertisement for Alpha-Radium cream. Another promised to 'rejuvenate the skin and activate the growth of the new cells needed to replace tired old cells', using a dosage that had, they claimed, been authorized by the Curie Institute. The Radior brand, on sale in the hairdressing departments of Harrods, Selfridges, and Whiteley's department stores in London, appeared on vanishing cream, hair tonic, and shampoo powder products that contained actual radium. The new element was even incorporated into radioactive wool used for baby clothes: 'When knitting your baby's underclothes, blankets, and sweaters, use O-Radium wool, precious source of heat and vital energy, resistant to shrinkage and

Advertisements for radiation-enhanced products

matting.'[70] From the restorative powers of such creams to the promise of a cure for cancer did not seem too great a leap. Curietherapy was the term coined to describe the treatment of tumours by exposure to radium, or, more usually, the gaseous emanation of radium that we now call radon.

Radium also appealed to amateur scientists, encouraged by popular books on the subject that appeared soon after the Curies first published their results. These stories of science-in-the-making presented the new discovery as an accessible piece of nature's wonder that could be experimented with at home. In a typical popularization of 1904, entitled *The Becquerel Rays and the Properties of Radium* by the Honourable R J Strutt, the author suggests several experiments the interested reader can undertake with a minimum of trouble. 'An interesting example of fluorescence under Becquerel rays is afforded by the tissues of the eye itself. The effect is easily observed. Close the eye and cover it with black paper, so as to exclude all light from without. Now bring up the radium outside. Distinct luminosity will be perceived, owing to the fluorescence of the tissues under the Becquerel rays, which penetrated the paper and the closed eyelid.'[71]

Strutt includes an appendix summarizing 'Madame Curie's account of the process' and advice on where to buy radium, which was by 1904 a rare but obtainable commodity. 'For most of the experiments, some radium will be required,' he writes. 'This may now be purchased from the majority of instrument makers; advertisements of radium and other requisites for experiments on radioactivity are to be seen in the scientific journals, notably in *Nature*. Five milligrams of pure radium bromide is a useful quantity. Such quantities are sold for about 5 pounds, though the price fluctuates very much at present. The salt is usually sold in a small capsule, which had a removable lid; for most of the experiments the lid is best left on.'[72]

Best to keep the lid on indeed. It is hard not to cringe at Strutt's eye experiment and the other parlour experiments he suggests. Today's permissible doses of radiation are minuscule compared with Strutt's five-milligram sample. At the time, the dangers of radium were thought to be limited to the surface burns sustained by men such as Rutherford and Becquerel, who often carried a vial of the element in a convenient waistcoat pocket. Pierre Curie performed some early experiments on himself after suffering from similar burns but in spite of his findings that the burns he inflicted on himself took months to heal and left permanent grey scars and in spite of the pain in his fingers and legs, Pierre never linked his exposure to radium with more systemic illness. Pierre's description of his self-experiments shows the seriousness of some of his symptoms. 'The extremities of the fingers which have held tubes or capsules containing very active products become hard and sometimes very painful; with one of us, the inflammation of the extremities of the fingers lasted about a fortnight and ended by the scaling of the skin, but their painful sensitiveness had not yet completely disappeared at the end of two months.'[73]

Marie Curie, who worked for nearly 40 years with radium and X-ray radiation and suffered from debilitating illnesses ranging from anaemia to kidney infections and serious cataracts, never ceased to advocate frequent bouts in the countryside as a cure for any fatigue due to overwork. It was 1924 before she installed anything other than the standard chemical protections in her laboratory. Rather than investigating radium's power to do harm, Marie promoted its medicinal uses. Early

Ionizing radiation damages biological tissues by bumping electrons out of their normal orbits. These free electrons – also called ions, hence 'ionizing radiation' – can then go on to disrupt other atoms, changing their atomic structure and causing normal molecular bonds to break. If the doses are high enough, cell damage can result and even low levels of radiation can cause the growth of cancers. If the free electrons damage the cells' DNA, genetic mutations may be introduced.

HEALTH RISKS

researchers experimented with radium as a tool for cancer treatment; its radiation killed diseased cells more readily than healthy cells, curing growths and certain tumours. It was also used as a dermatological tool: by partially destroying the skin, it caused new, apparently healthier skin to grow back.

Though it was still a recent discovery, the potential financial rewards to be gained from radium were clear. Doctors were expressing interest in the treatments, industrialists hoped to produce and sell radium for a profit in commercial spheres, even scientists wishing to investigate the new phenomena represented a potential market. But at this time Marie and Pierre decided together that they would not patent their purification process, a decision as unusual then as it would be today. *In agreement with me*, Marie wrote, *Pierre Curie decided to take no material profit from our discovery; in consequence we took out no patent and we have published the results of our research without reserve, as well as the processes of preparation of radium.*[74]

'YOU MUST NOT TALK OF PHYSICS WHILE YOU EAT'

This period of discovery, described by Curie as *the best and happiest years of our life, devoting our entire days to our work*, was also a time of fatigue and grief.[75] Curie lost 15 pounds (7 kilograms) in the five years following her discovery of radium. Her responsibilities at this time were numerous. With Pierre's aging father Eugène living with them, the household required more space than their three-room flat in the Latin Quarter afforded. They moved to a new house on boulevard Kellerman in the outskirts of Paris with a big garden that Irène could play in, but it was expensive at 4,000 francs a year. Pierre was earning just 500 francs a month and the higher rent and additional expenses of a servant and nurse to help with Irène meant that the family's funds were tight. *We have to be very careful*, Marie wrote to her brother in 1899, *and my husband's salary is not quite enough for us to live on, but up to now we have had some unexpected*

Marie, Irène, and Pierre in the garden of the house on Boulevard Kellerman. At 4,000 francs a year, the house stretched the Curies' household budget

extra resources every year, which keep us from having a deficit.[76] The 3,800-franc *prix Gegner*, awarded to Marie by the Academy of Sciences in July 1898 in recognition of her work on magnetism in steel and radioactivity, was one of the unexpected extras that helped supplement their income.

After reluctantly applying for, and failing to attain, a chair in physical chemistry at the Sorbonne (his unorthodox education and lack of connections conspired against him), Pierre was offered a post at the University of Geneva. The offer was a good one, paying nearly twice his salary at the EPCI and including the directorship of a laboratory, two assistants, and money to buy equipment. But nervous about taking too much time away from work for teaching, Pierre turned it down. Instead, he took another job as a lecturer for the newly established *certificat d'études* (study certificate) in physics, chemistry, and natural history, which was now a requirement for medical students. Marie supplemented the family income with her first salaried position, becoming the first woman on the faculty of

FINANCIAL STRUGGLES

the *École normale supérieure* (Higher teaching college) in Sèvres, where the best women teachers in France were trained. She introduced hands-on physics and chemistry courses, the first of their kind in France, that put experiments into the students' own hands in contrast to traditional teaching by demonstration and rote-learning. Eugénie Feytis, a young student of Curie's, remembered how 'often she brought us equipment made or modified by her which we used with her. It was very simple equipment but our guide was so skilled that we ended by achieving our measurements, and nothing was more fascinating than discussing the results we had in common with her after the bell . . . it would often happen that the pretty face of our teacher, so grave ordinarily, would brighten into an amused and charming smile after certain of our remarks.'[77] The Curies travelled as well, taking a medley of bicycle trips in France, to the Cévennes, the coast off the Channel from Le Havre to St Valery-sur-Somme, Le Pouldu, Arromanches, Le Tréport, and St Trojean. A trip to Poland allowed Pierre to practise his Polish and the young family to visit the sanatorium that Bronia was building in the Carpathian mountain town of Zakopane.

At the urging of a colleague, Pierre even put forward his name as a candidate for a vacant seat in the Academy of Sciences though he was opposed to the excessively ritualized institution and more generally to the awarding of honours for work that he felt should be pursued for its inherent interest. He reluctantly made the formal rounds of the homes of the 58 members of the Academy, leaving visiting cards when no one was in. His candidacy was unsuccessful.

Meanwhile, Marie's busy routine was taking its toll. George Sagnac, a young colleague of the Curies, wrote Pierre a letter expressing his concern over the change in Marie's appearance and urging both of them to slow down. 'I have been struck, when I have seen Mme Curie at the Society of Physics, by the alteration in her appearance. I know very well that she is overworked because of her thesis . . . You hardly eat at all, either of you. More than once I have seen Mme Curie nibble two slices of sausage and swallow a cup of tea with it. Do you think even a robust constitution would not suffer from such insufficient nourishment? What would become of you if Mme Curie lost her health? . . . It is necessary not to mix scientific preoccupations continually into every instant of your life, as you are doing. You must allow your body to breathe. You must sit down in peace before your meals and swallow them slowly, keeping away from talk about distressing things or simply things that tire the mind. You must not talk of physics while you eat . . .'[78] It is unlikely that Marie or Pierre heeded this advice. Events outside their control soon conspired to veil these years, so happy in the laboratory, so full of talk of physics, with the shadow of grief.

The first sad news came by letter. Marie's father was ill with gallstones and had had a bad fall. Marie immediately set out on the two-and-a-half day trip to Warsaw, but it was too late. On 14 May 1902, while Curie was en route to see him, Wladislaw Sklodowska died at the age of 70. He had lived to hear the initial reports of his daughter's successful isolation of radium and this offered some consolation to Curie. *My father who in his own youth had wished to do scientific work,* she wrote later, *was consoled in our separation by the progressive success of my work. I keep a tender memory of his kindness.*[79] In July, some happy news was reported. Marie Curie had a firm result from her years of work on the isolation of radium: a value for the atomic weight of radium of 225.

In the months following her father's death, Curie wrote up her long-deferred dissertation. She defended it in June of the following year before examiners who had taught her as a student at the Sorbonne: Gabriel Lippman and the chemist and future Nobel laureate Henri Moissan. She was duly awarded the title of doctor of physical sciences with the mention *très honorable* (that is, with distinction) and her thesis was published immediately as a cogent summary of the current state of the field of radioactivity. Ernest Rutherford turned up at the celebratory dinner that evening at the home of the Curies' colleague Paul Langevin. As he often did, Pierre Curie had brought along some radium in a vial coated with zinc sulphide. The guests gathered in the garden after dinner to see the spectacle. 'The luminosity was brilliant in the darkness', Rutherford remembered, 'and it was a splendid finale to an unforgettable day.'[80]

But then came another blow. Just two months later, in August 1903, Marie suffered a miscarriage in her fifth month of pregnancy. She felt the loss of the child keenly. *I am in such consternation over this accident that I have not had the courage to write to anybody,* she wrote to her sister Bronia. *I had grown so accustomed to the idea of the child that I am absolutely desperate and cannot be consoled. Write to me, I beg of you, if you think I should blame this on my general fatigue – for I must admit that I have not spared my strength. I had confidence in my constitution, and at present I regret this bitterly, as I have paid dear for it. The child – a little girl – was in good condition and was living. And I had wanted it so badly!*[81]

'CONIUNCTA VALENT'

In the midst of this difficult period, the Curies were propelled into international celebrity. Though she would grow in her later years to appreciate the recognition and special treatment that fame brought, initially Marie was as despairing of it as Pierre. The earlier newspaper articles on their discovery of radium were nothing compared with what was coming. Thanks to a letter from Gösta Mittag-Leffler, an influential member of the Swedish Academy of Sciences and also a fan of Marie's, Pierre knew that the committee had considered awarding the Nobel Prize in Physics to him and Henri Becquerel. He had written back, urging Mittag-Leffler to push for the nomination of Marie as well. 'If it is true that one is seriously thinking about me, I very much wish to be considered together with Madame Curie with respect to our research on radioactive bodies.'[82]

In late 1903, after a behind-doors intrigue that almost saw Marie Curie deprived of the prize in favour of her husband, the two learned that they had been awarded half of the Nobel Prize in physics for that year. Henri Becquerel, the original discoverer of radioactivity, was awarded the other half. On this occasion, the anti-establishment Pierre did not shun what was a great and formal honour for both himself and his wife. But both Curies seemed to distance themselves wilfully from what was already, in just the third year of its existence, a prize of major international standing, if not yet as prestigious as it is today.

It is only in the fourth paragraph of a letter written to her brother the day after the formal award ceremony had taken place that Marie shares the news: *We have been given half of the Nobel Prize. I do not know exactly what that represents; I believe it is about seventy thousand francs. For us, it is a huge sum. I don't know when we shall get the money, perhaps only when we go to Stockholm. We are obliged to lecture there during the six months following December 10th.* [83] Of the publicity, Marie wrote to her brother unhappily, *We are inundated with letters and with visits from photographers and journalists. One would like to dig into the ground somewhere to find a little peace. We have received a proposal from America to go there and give a series of lectures on our work. They ask us how much we want. Whatever the terms may be, we intend to refuse. With much effort we have avoided the banquets people wanted to organize in our honour. We refuse with the energy of despair, and people understand that there is nothing to be done.*[84] Pierre wrote to Carl Aurivillius, secretary of the Swedish Academy of Sciences, to thank him and to let him know that he and Marie could not make the trip to Stockholm to receive the medal and deliver the customary Nobel lecture. Their excessive teaching commitments and Marie Curie's ill health conspired to prevent them from coming. It would be three years before the Curies made it to Stockholm.

In his speech announcing the award, the President of the Royal Swedish Academy hailed the Curies as an exemplar of 'the old proverb, *coniuncta valent*, union is strength'. 'This makes us look at God's word in an entirely new light: "It is not good that the man should be alone; I will make him an help meet for him."'[85] His words seem patronizing today – after all, Marie and Pierre were jointly awarded a prize for work they had completed in equal measure. But given the controversy and political infighting that had marked the nomination process, it seems something of a miracle that Marie Curie was awarded the prize at all.

The Curies' aversion to publicity did not keep the press from making them a national sensation in France. If the Nobel committee had faltered in its decision to award Marie Curie the prize, they soon learned just how much esteem the female scientist would bring to their institution. The scientific coupling of Marie and Pierre caught the public's imagination. The story of the Curies' backbreaking isolation of radium was retold and once again journalists made faithful pilgrimages to the original shed on rue Lhomond at the EPCI. One reporter's summary for *La Semaine* (*The Week*) captures the excitable response to the award. 'Voilà perpetual motion, the eternal sun, the supreme inexhaustible force has at last been found through the geniuses of the inventors M. et Mme. Curie, whose Nobel Prize fits them like hand in glove."[86]

'A KIND OF STUPOR'

Pierre could hardly have disagreed more: 'I have wanted to write to you for a long time', he told his friend Georges Gouy in a letter from January 1904. 'Excuse me if I have not done so. The cause is the stupid life which I lead at present. You have seen this sudden infatuation for radium, which has all the advantages of a moment of popularity. We have been pursued by journalists and photographers from all countries of the world . . . With such a state of things I feel myself invaded by a kind of stupor.'[87]

Pierre's stupor was only partly caused by fame. He was also suffering from the physical effects of working with radiation. Searing pain in his legs, burnt and brittle fingers, and general fatigue were keeping him from the work he loved. 'I am neither very well nor very ill,' he wrote Gouy. 'But I get tired easily, and I no longer have more than a very feeble capacity for work. My wife, on the contrary, leads a most active life, between her children, the school at Sèvres and the laboratory. She does not lose a minute, and attends much more regularly than I do to the progress of the laboratory, in which she passes the greater part of her day.'[88] Indeed, Marie Curie seemed to have a high level of resistance to the damaging radioactivity she worked with. Though she was often fatigued, she did not experience the acute symptoms reported by Pierre.

Reluctantly, Pierre applied once again for membership of the Academy of Sciences. He made the formal rounds, leaving visiting cards at houses where no one was home, corners folded down. The protocol rewarded itself, if only barely, when Pierre, now a Nobel laureate, was elected in 1905 by a margin of just eight votes.

Pierre was unenthused. In letter after letter to his close friend Georges Gouy he reveals his abiding discomfort with the institution and the role he felt forced to play there. 'I went to the institute on Monday, but I really must say I don't know what I was doing there. I have nothing to do with any of the members, and the interest of the meetings is null. I feel very clearly that these circles are not mine.'[89]

The Nobel Prize had brought money to the Curies but it had not yet changed the physical space in which they worked. It was only in late 1904 that a new professorship was finally created at the Sorbonne for Pierre. Marie, despite being an equal partner in the Nobel Prize that had led to this post, was appointed as Pierre's assistant. It was the first time in her life she would be paid a salary for her work. Both waited expectantly for the promised laboratory to be constructed. Throughout this time, Marie and Pierre maintained a close and affectionate working relationship. Their assistant, Albert Laborde, would later remember one incident in particular: 'I was working with a mercury apparatus. Pierre Curie was there. Mme Curie came, grew interested in the mechanism, and at first did not understand. The detail was, for that matter, very simple. Nevertheless, when the explanation was given she insisted upon refuting it. Then Pierre Curie launched out with a happy, tender, indignant "Well, really, Marie – !" which remained in my ears, and of which I wish I could convey the nuance.'[90]

Meanwhile, Marie was pregnant again. This time the pregnancy, though difficult, was successful. A second daughter, Eve, was born on 6 December 1904. From the start, Eve was different from Irène. *The children are growing well,* Marie wrote to her brother. *Little Eve sleeps very little, and protests energetically if I leave her lying awake in her cradle. As I am not a stoic, I carry her in my arms until she grows quiet. She does not resemble Irène. She has dark hair and blue eyes, whereas up to now Irène has rather light hair and green-brown eyes.*[91] Marie recorded her children's progress in a domestic notebook that serves as a counterpoint to her laboratory notebooks. Steps taken, teeth lost, weight gained, and foods eaten are recorded with the scrupulous detail of a trained experimentalist.

Marie's schedule, as Pierre had noted to his friend Gouy, was unforgiving. *I resumed teaching at Sèvres on the first of February,* she told her brother. *In the afternoons I am at the laboratory and in the mornings at home, except for two mornings a week spent at Sèvres . . . I have a great deal of work, what with the housekeeping, the children, the teaching and the laboratory, and I don't know how I shall manage it all.*[92]

But she managed to find the time and energy in June of 1905 to make the long-deferred trip to Stockholm with Pierre, where, though the Curies had been jointly awarded half of the prize, Pierre gave the lecture required by the committee. In it he offered a famous and rare pronouncement on the potential effects of their discovery. 'It might even be thought that radium could become very dangerous in criminal hands, and here the question can be raised whether mankind benefits from knowing the secrets of Nature, whether it is ready to profit from it or whether this knowledge will not be harmful for it . . . I am among those who believe with Nobel that humanity will obtain more good than evil from future discoveries.'[93]

A mind uninhibited enough to think new thoughts may also think foolish ones. Pierre was insightful about possible future uses and abuses of radioactivity but he also held views that are today considered pseudo-scientific at best. What should we make of Pierre's confession that he has been attending séances hosted by an Italian-born psychic who entered trance-like states during which a 'hole' in her head emitted a cold breeze? 'We have had some more séances with the medium Eusapia Palladino. The result is that these phenomena really exist and it is no longer possible for me to doubt it,' he wrote Georges Gouy. 'It's improbable but this is so and it is *impossible to deny it* after the séances we have had in perfectly controlled conditions. A kind of fluid member detaches from the medium (mostly from her arms and legs . . .) and pushes objects forcefully. (Richet calls these *exoplasmes*) . . . How do you explain these displacements of objects from a distance, how do you conceive that the thing is possible? There is here, in my opinion, a whole domain of entirely new facts and physical states in space of which we have no conception.'[94] Pierre wrote these words just two days before his death. His willingness to remain open to the seemingly unbelievable had led him, with Marie, into the inner world of the atom. It had also led him to the threshold of a supernatural world of ectoplasm and telekinesis. The gentle and thoughtful man would not live to explore either.

Death and Laboratory Life · 1906–1911

'What was he dreaming of this time?'

Pierre's father was home alone with Eve when they came to tell him. He knew as soon as he saw the grim-faced Paul Appell, head of the Faculty of Sciences, and Jean Perrin standing unannounced on his doorstep. 'My son is dead.'

'He is dead': the three words repeated to Marie when she finally returned from a day-trip with Irène. *Can one comprehend such words?* she later wrote in a journal. *Pierre is dead, he who I had seen leave looking fine this morning, he who I expected to press in my arms this evening. I will only see him dead and it's over for ever. I repeat your name again and always, 'Pierre, Pierre, Pierre, my Pierre,' alas that doesn't make him come back, he is gone for ever, leaving me nothing but desolation and despair.*[95]

Like a rebuke to his years of meditation, Pierre Curie's death came in an instant and without warning. Walking from a lunch for the Association of Professors in the Faculty of Science, Pierre was struck by a heavily laden horse-drawn carriage on rue Dauphine, just south of the Pont Neuf.

In her biography of her mother, Eve, who was just two years old at the time, re-creates the moments before her father's death: the rain that obscured his vision and the noise of tramcars and horse-drawn carriages in the crowded old streets south of the Pont Neuf. Pierre sought walking space where he could find it, on the pavement or in the street. He shifted from behind the shelter of a slow-moving cab. A horse-drawn carriage drew up quickly. 'The space between the two vehicles narrowed dizzily. Surprised, Pierre, in an awkward movement, attempted to hang on to the chest of the animal, which suddenly reared. The scientist's heels slipped on the wet pavement. A cry arose, made of a dozen shouts of horror: Pierre had fallen beneath the feet of the powerful horses. Pedestrians cried "Stop! Stop!" The driver pulled on the reins, but in vain. The team of horses kept on.'[96] In a few moments, it was over. Pierre's skull was crushed by the back wheel of the wagon. Loaded with six tonnes of cargo, it killed Pierre instantly. He was 47 years old, a husband, father of two, Sorbonne professor, and Nobel laureate. To Marie he was simply 'my Pierre'.

In the only journal she ever kept, Marie recorded her grief. *We put you into the coffin Saturday morning, and I held your head up for this move. We kissed your cold face for the last time. Then a few periwinkles from the garden on the coffin and the little picture of me that you called 'the good little student' and that you loved. It is the picture that must go with you into the grave, the picture of her who had the happiness of so pleasing you that you did not hesitate to offer to share your life with her, even when you had seen her only a few times. You often told me that this was the only occasion in your life when you acted without hesitation, with the absolute conviction that you were doing very well. My Pierre, I think you were not wrong. We were made to live together, and our union had to be.*

I put my head against [the coffin] . . . and in great distress . . . I spoke to you. I told you that I loved you and that I had always loved you with all my heart . . . I promised that I would never give another the place that you occupied in my life and that I would try to live as you would have wanted me to live. And it seemed to me that from this cold contact of my forehead with the casket something came to me, something like a calm and an intuition that I would find the courage to live. Was this an illusion or was this an accumulation of energy coming from you and condensing in the closed casket which came to me . . . as an act of charity on your part?[97]

We took you back to Sceaux, and we saw you go down into the big deep hole. Then the dreadful procession of people. They wanted to take us away. Jacques and I resisted. We wanted to see everything to the end. They filled the grave and put sheaves of flowers on it. Everything is over, Pierre is sleeping his last sleep beneath the earth; it is the end of everything, everything, everything.[98]

'AN INFINITE SADNESS'

Marie moved, with her children and her father-in-law, to a house in Sceaux, which was more peaceful than the house on boulevard Kellerman and did not contain painful memories of life with Pierre. She rallied her spirits to attend to important financial matters. She also found time, in the weeks after Pierre's death, to correspond with his friend Georges Gouy about an experimental electrical circuit. Within days of Pierre's death, she was back at the laboratory, measuring, precipitating, and purifying. But she soon realized she had made a mistake. Pierre's presence saturated the two rooms on rue Cuvier. Her journal writing captures her ambivalence about the space and work that she had shared with Pierre for 11 years. *I tried to take a measurement for a curve on which each of us had made some points. But after some time I felt the impossibility of continuing. The laboratory had an infinite sadness and seemed a desert.*[99] *The moments of calm are rare, and the feeling of obsessive distress reigns,* she confided to her journal, *with some moments of anguish, and also uneasiness, and sometimes the absurd idea that all that is an illusion and that you are coming back.*[100]

As time passed the attention that the laboratory demanded and the satisfaction the work gave her began to effect a change. The intricacies of the work that had always given her great gratification offered one way forward into an otherwise bleak future. *I work in the laboratory all my days. I am better there than anywhere else. I feel more and more that my life with you, Pierre, is irrevocably over . . . I can't conceive any more of anything that could give me true personal joy except perhaps scientific work — and even there — no, because if I succeeded with it, I could not endure you not to know it.*[101]

The biggest professional change was her appointment, two weeks after Pierre's death, to an assistant professorship at the Sorbonne, where she occupied Pierre's old chair. Her salary rose from 2,400 to 10,000 francs and she became the first female professor in France, attaining full rank within two years. Though her suffering was profound, there is no doubt that Marie gained power and prestige after Pierre's death. She would most likely never have been appointed to a professorship at the Sorbonne while Pierre was alive. Those who hoped for a spectacle from Curie were frustrated. In her inaugural lecture, Marie picked up, to the sentence, where Pierre had left off. *When one considers the progress that has been made in physics in the past ten years, one is surprised at the advance that has taken place in our ideas concerning electricity and matter . . .*[102] Ignoring journalists and the curious public alike, she proceeded, nervously at first but with increasing confidence, through her lecture.

Marie Curie's personal life, jealously guarded before Pierre's death, became almost monastic in the immediate aftermath. In addition to her children and Pierre's father, she saw only Pierre's brother Jacques, and her close friend Henriette Perrin, the wife of Jean. As a single working mother, she struggled to put in a full day at the laboratory, direct her children's education, and keep the household in order. Her health, never reliable at the best of times, caused her more grief. In a letter to her old childhood friend Kazia, she shared some of her anxieties. *I was not able to see your protégé, Monsieur K. The day when he came, I was very unwell, which is often the case, and also I had a lecture to give the next day.*[103] Eve gives a sharp portrait of her grieving mother as seen from a child's perspective: 'One of my earliest childhood memories is that of my mother collapsing to the floor in a faint, in the dining-room at Sceaux — and of her pallor, her mortal inertia.'[104]

Following Pierre's death, the public perception of Marie shifted from devoted scientific helpmate to scientific saint. In photographs she is often portrayed alone, caught in a pose of intense concentration. A typical image shows her standing in a sparsely furnished laboratory wearing a high-necked floor-length black dress. She looks away from the camera in the direction of a nearby apparatus, though her gaze is softened and she seems, in fact, to be staring off into space. The door behind her is closed, and the walls are bare save for what look like measuring devices. Though it is obviously staged, it looks as if the portrait was taken when Curie was unaware, lost in the dream-like reverie that she had so admired in Pierre.

Despite her penchant for solitude and her alarming fatigue, Curie soon turned her attention to another pressing problem. Her children were growing – Irène was nine and Eve was three – and she began to worry over their education. For this over-achieving daughter of schoolteacher parents, it is not surprising schooling was important. What seems remarkable, given her own ferocious work ethic, is that Curie believed in the value of a moderate educational regime. Children, she declared, should not be imprisoned in school. Too much time engaged in classroom memorization and too little time in the fresh air were no good for young minds. Their lives should be an active balance of physical and intellectual exertion.

Marie Curie gathered together her friends at the Sorbonne for

Marie with Eve and Irène in 1908

an unusual venture in cooperative home education. The parent-teachers were an eclectic and distinguished lot. Along with Marie herself, the physicist Paul Langevin, the physical chemist Jean Perrin, and the naturalist Henri Mouton all signed up to teach science and mathematics. Mrs Chavannes, the wife of a professor at the College of France taught English and German. The sculptor Magrou taught art. Classes for the ten lucky children of the ambitious educators took place in houses scattered in various Paris suburbs and in the laboratories of the Sorbonne. One day Marie caught Irène daydreaming and threw her notebook out the window when Irène could not answer a normally easy question. Startled, Irène ran to retrieve her notebook and on her return to the classroom promptly answered the question.

Of the friends and colleagues involved in this educational experiment, one would become a special confidant over the next few years. Paul Langevin was an old friend of the Curies. He had come to study under Pierre at the EPCI when he was just 17 years old. Like Marie, he had excelled in formal education, taking first in his class at the elite *École normale supérieure*. In 1897, he received the first research scholarship awarded to a non-British scientist at the Cavendish Laboratory in Cambridge and studied there for a year under its director J J Thomson, then about to announce his discovery of the electron. When Pierre was appointed to his chair at the Sorbonne following the award of the Nobel Prize, it was natural for Langevin to succeed him as professor at the EPCI. Langevin's research interests overlapped with Pierre's, including work on magnetism, and extended into investigating the relationship between mass and energy – for which another man is today much more famous. Shortly after Langevin's death in 1946 Albert Einstein paid the French scientist the ultimate compliment: 'It seems to be certain that he would have developed the special theory of relativity if that had not been done elsewhere, for he had clearly recognized its essential points.'[105] Indeed Langevin was one of the first in France to promote Einstein's theory, providing an early defence of it in an anti-German environment.

Langevin's close friendship with Pierre must have been important to Marie. He was someone who could truly understand what she had lost. He himself was suffering in an unhappy marriage to Jeanne Desfosses, with whom he had four children. At first, he confided his marriage troubles to Henriette Perrin, who in turn shared them with Marie Curie. For her part, Curie confided to her friend Marguerite Borel (the daughter of the head of the Faculty of Sciences Paul Appell and the wife of mathematician Emile Borel) that she was worried for Langevin. She feared that he might give up his pursuit of pure science and cede to the pressure of a diffi-

Paul Langevin

cult marriage. 'He is sad,' she told Marguerite. 'He is weak. You and I are strong. He needs understanding, sweet affection.'[106]

By 1907 Langevin had discovered for himself Curie's sympathetic qualities. In an undated document held at the EPCI, Langevin explains that he was drawn to her 'as to a light, in the sanctuary of mourning in which she was enclosed, with a fraternal affection born of the friendship for her and her husband, brought close

because of the common lessons we were giving our children . . . Little by little, I got in the habit of talking to her of the difficulties of my existence, which I had always kept quiet from my friends, and I began to seek from her a little of the tenderness which I missed at my house.'[107] In this way began a relationship that would deepen beyond friendship into a full-blown affair, with Curie and Langevin meeting for trysts at a flat they rented on rue Banquier near the Sorbonne.

During the years following Pierre's death, as Curie searched to find new ways of being in the world, she took her children on long summer holidays to the seaside for the bouts of fresh air she believed to be crucial to good health. *The air is very gentle and very good there* she wrote of the beach at Arromanches.[108] After spending some weeks with her children, she returned to Paris each summer before them, leaving them in the care of a governess and relatives. Letters written during these periods reveal Irène, aged nine to twelve years old, testing the boundaries of her mother's attentiveness and jockeying for recognition. 'I would like to know if Mé [her pet name for her mother] will take some [sea baths] and what day you will come, on what train, and if that will be soon.'[109] For her part, Marie kept careful track of her children's progress in her notebooks. In 1908 she wrote of Irène that she *Looks very good. Good swim and bath daily. Bicycle trip of 50 kilometres.* Eve, aged five, is in *excellent condition* and *grew several centimetres during the summer.*[110]

A STRATEGY OF ACCUMULATION

Given Curie's combination of a crushing grief, relentless work, two young children to tend to, and nearly ten years of exposure to damaging radiation, part of the inertia that the young Eve noticed in her mother was certainly physical. But was there another kind of inertia in Curie's life, despite her drive and her ambition? Some historians of science have asserted that Marie Curie stopped producing novel results when her husband died. It is true that Curie was not so concerned with the theoretical ramifications of her work. But she was intensely interested in the practical uses of radioactivity in science, medicine, and industry. Perhaps it would be fairer to say that after Pierre's death, Curie's focus shifted from pure scientific research and laboratory process to the practical, institutional, and political implications of her discoveries.

Increasing commercial demand and a rich stream of important research papers on radioactivity meant that radium was at the centre of a growing interdisciplinary field. In order to harness the power of her discoveries on the international scene and ensure that her laboratory retained its prominent position in the world of radio-activity, Curie focused on accumulating as much radium as possible. One logical consequence of this 'strategy of accumulation', in the words of historian Soraya Boudia, was Curie's commitment to creating particular standards of measurement in the new science of radioelements.

By 1906 there was an international consensus that some sort of standard measure of radioactivity was needed. With a proper standard the results of different laboratories could be compared, doctors could begin to establish benchmark doses of radiation for cancer therapy, and geologists and hydrologists studying radio-activity in the earth's crust could communicate more effectively. The novel discipline of radioactivity itself would benefit from a shared standard as a mark of social as well as scientific cohesion.

Marie Curie's attitude towards an international standard was shaped by the activity of her laboratory. For one thing, she wanted it to be based on radium rather than any other radioactive element. Since radium was chemically the best understood of these elements – thanks in large part to the work of her laboratory – this was not unreasonable and radium was chosen to act as the basis of a standard at the 1910 International Congress on Electricity and Radiology held in Brussels and attended by Curie and Rutherford.

Defining the unit of measurement was trickier. Curie was ill when the members of the special International Commission for the Radium Standard gave her name to a unit used to measure radio-activity, based on the amount of gas that emanated from a very small quantity of 10^{-12} grams of radium. This tiny unit was well suited

A typical portrait of Curie: solitary, serious and in the workplace

to workers such as doctors and geologists, who typically dealt with small amounts of radioactive material. But Curie, used to dealing in much larger quantities, was unimpressed and objected through her colleague André Debierne: 'Madame Curie wants a change in the propositions adopted yesterday evening. The more important emanation unit and the more useful one for physicists is the quantity of emanation in equilibrium with one gram of radium. Marie Curie would prefer to keep the name Curie for this unit which would be commonly employed in the radioactivity laboratories.'[111] At the cost of alienating those scientists who did not appreciate her doctrinaire approach, Curie won the battle. The standard would be based on a gram of radium and Curie would prepare it.

In 1911 Marie Curie duly prepared a glass tube containing 21.99 milligrams of pure radium chloride. It was subsequently compared with multiple standards created by the skilled chemist Otto Hönigschmid. The match was good and Curie's sample was deemed a worthy international standard. But only after considerable prodding by Rutherford, who insisted that the Commission could not allow the international standard to remain in private hands, did Curie relinquish it to the *Bureau International des Poids et Mesures* (International Office of Weights and Measures) for safe-keeping. Uneasy at letting go of hard-won radium, even to an august body such as the *Bureau International*, Curie at least had the consolation prize of a measurements service established in her laboratory.

The measurements service ensured that the Curie laboratory had an ongoing role in the application of the international radium standard. Much as the Cavendish Laboratory in Cambridge had done for electrical units such as the ohm and the amp in the 1870s, the Curie laboratory assigned and maintained standard values in radioactivity, based on the international standards that Curie had played a large role in defining. It took Curie four years to gain official approval for the measurement service from the university administrators, who felt that she gave preferential treatment to her old friend Armet de Lisle.

Once the service was established, the marketers of radioactive products came to the Curie laboratory to determine the strength of their samples. For a fee they received a numbered certificate stating the measurements taken. These certificates were meant to staunch the flow of unauthorized advertisements for radioactive products. Customers included the makers of medical devices and cosmetic products, geologists, and would-be spa owners. The Curie laboratory performed these services from 1911 to Marie Curie's death in 1934.

Scandal · 1911–1914

'WHAT A PRETTY HAT THE CUPOLA WOULD MAKE'

Despite her successful preparation of the standard sample for the curie, 1911 would prove to be Marie's worst year since the loss of Pierre. Early in the year, she consented to having her name put forward for nomination to the Academy of Sciences. The most powerful organization in French science admitted new members only on the death of an existing member. Chemist and physicist Désiré Gernez had died in October 1910. Curie, a Nobel laureate and a member of the Polish, Czech, Swedish, and Dutch academies, the American Philosophical Society, and the Imperial Academy in St Petersburg was notably absent from France's most prestigious scientific body.

Applying for membership was out of character for Marie Curie, who viewed formal honours with the same disdain as her husband had. But Pierre's first, abortive candidacy was fresh in both Marie Curie's and the Academy's memory and perhaps she wanted to vindicate his name. She may have had a very practical reason for applying as well, as members of the Academy had ready access to publication in *Comptes rendus (Reports)*, the Academy's house journal. *Comptes rendus* had a conveniently speedy publication policy: articles appeared just five days after the Academy's weekly meeting.

The Academy accepted three candidates for the seat left vacant by Gernez: Marie Curie, Edouard Branly, and Marcel Brillouin. That Curie was considered at all was a bold move for the all-male institution, despite the fact that she was by 1911 one of the leading

Mockery of Curie's candidacy: the Academy of Sciences, with caricature showing a woman frivolously wearing the Academy's cupola as a hat

physicists in France. Her main competitor was to be Branly, known as the father of wireless telegraphy in France and championed by his supporters for developing a technology that rescued many at sea. The solid but comparatively unexceptional Brillouin did not pose a threat.

While Pierre had actively disliked the stiff formality of the Academy election process, Marie Curie was simply unmoved by it. Her impassivity was to be a cause of regret. She had underestimated the extent of the mistrust and ill will that the French establishment felt towards her. Her fame, her gender, and her uncompromising attitude conspired to alienate her from the powerful men who saw it as their duty to guard the holy of holies of French science. Curie did have supporters, men such as her old teacher at the Sorbonne, Gabriel Lippmann, who lobbied hard to get her elected. But Branly had an equally powerful lobby. As an elderly scientist who had developed wireless telegraphy in France and recently missed out on a share of the Nobel physics prize, Branly cut a sympathetic figure.

In the first few weeks of January, Curie and her competitors undertook the required house calls to members of the Academy, the very visits that Pierre had resented so much. In the meantime the press had taken up the story. Curie's good works for France – the discovery of radium, the Nobel Prize, her collaborative marriage with a great French scientist – were no guarantee against the criticism of the right-wing, nationalist, and religious writers who saw her as a threat to their ideal of France, a female gate-crasher at a very old party. A cartoon of the time in the conservative news-paper *Le Figaro* depicts a young woman with flowing tresses and an impressive décolletage wearing the famous cupola of the Academy on her head. 'What a pretty hat the Cupola would make', reads the caption.[112] The most objectifying representation of Marie appeared in the journal *Excelsior* which published a physiognomic and grapho-logical study of Curie, portraying her features in the stark style of a criminal's mug-shot. The scientist had become an object for (pseudo-)scientific study: the article and illustration presented Curie as a dangerous type, a specimen of perverted will and inappropriate ambition that could prove dangerous to the Academy.

On 23 January, after a few weeks of biting press coverage and back-stage manoeuvring, the Academy voted. The count was close: Branly had won, receiving 30 votes to Curie's 28. Though it was far from unusual for a candidate not to be accepted on the first try, Curie's defeat still stung. She received the telephone call in her laboratory and spoke not a word of it to any of her colleagues. But while she endeavoured, successfully if Eve's account can be trusted, to hide any disappointment from her colleagues, her resentment found other means of expression:

The female scientist as criminal

DENIED MEMBERSHIP

it would be eleven years before she published again in *Comptes rendus*.

Later that year the unpleasant publicity surrounding her candidacy for the Academy would seem mild. In the summer of 1911 Curie holidayed in Italy with her daughters, now twelve and six, before sending them to Poland to visit her sister Bronia at the tuberculosis sanatorium she had founded at Zakopane. By October she was on her way to Brussels to attend the first of what would become the celebrated Solvay Congresses. Funded by a Belgian industrial chemist, the all-expenses-paid conferences brought the best physicists in the world together for open discussion of current research. As Rutherford described it to his friend the Yale physicist Bertram Boltwood in his inimitable style: 'I am going at the end of next week to Brussels to take part in a small Congress, about fifteen people, on the Theory of Radiations. Some wealthy man in Brussels pays a thousand francs each for our expenses. This is the sort of Congress I have no objection to attending.'[113]

The roll call of this first meeting reads like a who's who of great scientists of the day. In a famous photograph of these first delegates, Marie sits at a table flanked by her former teacher Henri Poincaré and her friend Jean Perrin, who had first characterized cathode rays as streams of negatively charged particles. She rests her head on her hand in a pose of deep concentration, as if she and Poincaré are considering a problem. She is the only woman in the group. The other delegates face the camera, fashionable moustaches exuberantly waxed and gold watch chains gleaming across well-fed stomachs. Behind Poincaré stands a youthful Albert Einstein, his hair still dark and his moustache neatly trimmed. On his left, on the edge of the picture, is a serious-looking Paul Langevin, his moustache impressively twirled into tight tips. Among the physicists to Einstein's right are a hale-looking Rutherford and a wormy-looking Max Planck, whose work on the energy emitted by black bodies laid the foundation for quantum theory, X-ray spectroscopist Maurice

The first Solvay Congress, in 1911. Jean Perrin is on Curie's right; Henri Poincaré on her left. Ernest Rutherford is standing behind her; the three men on his left are Kamerlingh Onnes, Albert Einstein, and, at the edge of the picture, Paul Langevin. Solvay sits at the head of the table

Branded 'a sheer delight to diabolical Jesuits' by Einstein, the first Solvay Congress was held between 30 October and 3 November 1911 at the luxurious Hotel Métropole in Brussels. Belgian chemist and businessman Ernest Solvay invited the world's leading physicists to an all-expenses-paid discussion forum on the subject of 'Radiation and Quanta'. By focusing the attention of elite scientists on a particular topic, the congresses set the tone for a new way of doing physics in the 20th century. Key problems would be attacked by a small international group of self-selecting savants. The topics of the first congresses defined cutting-edge science for the time. From quanta and radiation in 1911, the congresses had moved on to the electron theory of matter by 1921 and by 1933 focused on the structure and properties of atomic nuclei. In providing a forum for discussing the fundamental questions – What is matter? What is energy? – the congresses helped foster an international approach to physics that was reductionist, theoretical and by invitation only. Though she was ostracized from some parts of the scientific world, Curie was a secure member of this international physics club. Despite frequent illness, she attended all seven Solvay Congresses held during her lifetime.

THE ELITE GATHERS

de Broglie and Dutch theoretical physicist H A Lorenz. At the head of the table sits a dapper, white-haired Ernest Solvay, radiating self-satisfaction: the magnanimous philanthropist among his collection of rare and valuable friends.

On 4 November 1911, just after this meeting of great scientific minds, the newspaper *Le Journal* broke the story under the headline 'A Story of Love. Mme Curie and Professor Langevin'. Marie Curie was a home-breaker tearing a father of four from his family with 'the fires of radium'. Incriminating correspondence between Curie and Langevin, allegedly in the hands of Madame Langevin, was mentioned. The details of the affair, if overblown, were essentially accurate. Within days the story was international, titillating newspaper readers from London to San Francisco.

In the same week Marie Curie received other important news. This time it arrived quietly, by telegram: 'Nobel Prize for chemistry awarded to you. Letter follows. Aurivillius.' It was the head of the Committee on Prizes writing to inform Marie Curie that she had become the first person, man or woman, to be awarded two Nobel Prizes. To this day, she remains the only person to have been awarded two Nobel science prizes in different subjects.

Some grumbled that Curie had effectively been awarded the same prize twice, since both prizes honoured her work on radioactivity. The wording of the awards was just different enough to squeak through. But for the time being, these doubts about scientific merit were completely overshadowed in both the public's eye and Curie's own by the news of her affair with Langevin.

Curie was deeply disturbed by the revelations about her relationship with Langevin. She issued a statement in the less hostile *Le Temps* newspaper that made her views crystal clear. *I consider all intrusions of the press and of the public into my private life as abominable*

. . . Henceforward I shall rigorously take action against all publication of writings attributed to me. At the same time I have the right to demand as damages considerable sums which will be used in the interests of science.[114]

Whatever the liberal rhetoric of the Third Republic and the risqué behaviour of the denizens of bohemian cafés on the left bank in Paris, France in 1911 was not ready to countenance a public affair. The Dreyfus affair of 1894, in which a Jewish army officer had been wrongly accused and convicted of espionage (he was exonerated in 1904), was still very much an open wound in French society, exposing the tension between the ideal of a liberal Republic and the reality of widespread anti-Semitism and bigotry. In this atmosphere the affair between Curie and Langevin became another chapter in the story of France's struggle against outsiders and infidels. Curie became Polish again. Madame Langevin obligingly played the role of victimized French womanhood.

Right-wing newspaper *L'Intransigeant* (*The Intransigent*) made light of fears that Curie would respond to the scandal by leaving France. Curie's scientific abilities were 'overrated'. The real concern should be for the 'French mother, who . . . wants only to keep her children . . . It is with this mother, not with the foreign woman, that the public sympathizes . . . This mother wants her children. She has some ammunition. She has some support. She has above all the eternal force of the truth on her side. She will triumph.'[115] The next day the paper added, 'All French mothers are on the side of the victim and against her persecutors.'[116]

Marie Curie issued a strong statement condemning the *mad extravagance* of the suggestion that she had 'disappeared' with Langevin when it was common knowledge among their colleagues that they had both been attending the conference in Brussels. *There is nothing in my acts which obliges me to feel diminished. I will not add anything.*[117]

In fact, the scandal surrounding her liaison with Paul Langevin had almost cost her the second Nobel Prize. The furore had reached the Swedish Academy just days before the planned announcement of the award. The Swedish ambassador to France was asked to look into the matter. He duly cabled back: 'The said lady and professor who have been interviewed both protest against the information [in the paper]. Seem to have been together at a scientific meeting in Brussels.'[118] The ambassador concluded that the mood among professional scientists was in favour of Marie Curie. This was all that was needed by Carl Aurivillius, still Swedish Academy secretary and a supporter of Curie's. Curie was awarded the prize, but the papers gave little prominence to it. They had a better story.

Many friends and colleagues wrote letters supporting Curie. Pierre's brother Jacques Curie was outraged. 'Doesn't one have the right to sue newspapers for damages?' he wanted to know. Langevin should have left his wife some time ago, he continued: 'she's a plague who has been profoundly hurtful to him during his entire existence since his marriage.'[119]

Einstein wrote privately to his friend Heinrich Zangger that he did not believe that Curie was 'either domineering or has some other such affliction. She is a straightforward, honest person whose duties and burdens are just too much for her.' Besides, he did not think Curie 'attractive enough to become dangerous for anyone'.[120] To Curie he wrote, 'I feel the need to tell you how much I have come to admire your spirit, your energy and your honesty. I consider myself fortunate to have made your personal acquaintance in Brussels . . . I will always be grateful that we have among us people like you – as well as Langevin – genuine human beings, in whose company one can rejoice. If the rabble continues to be occupied with you, simply stop reading that drivel. Leave it to the vipers it was fabricated for.'[121]

The American dancer Loie Fuller had first met Marie and Pierre years earlier, when she had contacted them to explore the possibility of incorporating luminous radium into her costumes and stage sets. (The Curies had politely informed her that it would not be feasible, but had maintained a friendship with the charming performer.) Now she wrote to lend her emotional support, 'I love you, I take your two hands in mine and I love you. Pay no attention to the lies, *c'est la vie.*'[122]

At the heart of the scandal were letters reputed to be between Marie Curie and Paul Langevin. Curie's most powerful friends rallied to her cause, using their considerable influence to try to block their publication through the Paris Press Syndicate. Their actions may have bought time, but could not stop the inevitable. On 23 November 1911, long extracts from the letters were published in the *L'Oeuvre* newspaper under the title 'The Sorbonne Scandals'. It is unclear how authentic these extracts are. The provenance of the letters written by Langevin to Curie is uncertain, since the letters had supposedly been retrieved from Langevin's desk by a private detective hired by a jealous and increasingly agitated Madame Langevin, who had gone so far as to threaten to kill Curie if she did not leave France. Would Paul Langevin have saved a copy of his own letters to Curie? None of the dates on the letters is complete. It is also clear that Gustave Téry, the publisher of *L'Oeuvre*, edited the letters to make them appear as incriminating as possible. Nevertheless the excerpts, even if unflatteringly presented, contain details and are written in a style that suggest that they are authentic. They have been treated as such in most biographies of Curie.

The letters, which were said to date from the summer of 1910, are not salacious by modern standards, but they are the record of an intimate, sexual relationship. Langevin wrote to Curie of his problems at home and she responded with passionate jealousy, sharp advice and tender words. *But when I know that you are with her, my nights are atrocious, I can't sleep, I manage with great difficulty to sleep two or three hours; I wake up with a sensation of fever and can't work.*

Don't ever come down [from the upstairs bedroom] *unless she comes to look for you, work late . . . As for the pretext that you were looking for, tell her that, working late and rising early, you absolutely have need of rest in order to be able to do your work, that her requirement of a common bed unnerves you and makes it impossible for you to have a real rest.*

We are joined by a deep affection which we ought not to allow to be destroyed . . . What couldn't we extract from this instinctive and so spontaneous sentiment, which is so consistent with our rights and compatible with our intellectual needs, to which it's so beautifully adapted? I believe we've extracted a great deal: some good shared work, a good solid friendship, courage in our life, and even more beautiful children of our love, in the best accepted sense of that word.[123]

In a long letter that was to prove central to the case against her, Curie cautions Langevin not to get his wife pregnant during a period of reconciliation. For the press this advice was tantamount to treason. Would Curie deny France its rightful progeny, needed to keep the German threat at bay? Paradoxically, at the same time as they indicted Curie for the passion she shared with Langevin, the press also found fault with what they took to be her overly detached tone in the letters, a tone that Jacques Curie had approvingly labelled as 'scientific'.[124] 'This foreign woman', wrote a journalist for *l'Action Française*, ' . . . claims to speak in the name of reason, in the name of a morally superior Life, of a transcendent Ideal underneath which she hides her monstrous egoism. From above, she disposes of these poor people: of the husband, of the wife, of the children . . . And she applies her scientist's subtlety in indicating the ingenious means by which one can torture this simple wife in order to make her desperate and to force the rupture.'[125] In a particularly caustic article, Gustave Téry, founder, editor, and main writer for *L'Oeuvre,* had called Langevin 'a boor and a coward'. The assault upon Langevin's honour and manhood had gone too far. The physicist challenged the journalist to a duel.

Duels were surprisingly common in this period, if stylized

and occasionally absurd. Langevin and Téry's duel was ultimately ridiculous. Despite his previous rants against Langevin, when confronted with a man who was undoubtedly one of France's great scientists Téry fell back on platitudes. 'It is impossible to kill a man as worthy as Langevin.' He never raised his pistol. Langevin raised his but did not fire. 'I am not an assassin. I will not shoot either.'[126]

Though the Curie-Langevin affair was to inspire five (non-fatal) duels, the scandal was eventually put to rest by mutual agreement between the Langevins. Paul Langevin agreed to separate from his wife and relinquish custody of his four children, with the understanding that he would be responsible for their intellectual development. For Curie, the brief affair was the last intimate relationship she would have with a man and the beginning of a year of serious illness. She and Langevin would eventually take up their old friendship outside the public eye and almost certainly without any of their former intimacy.

After the duel between Téry and Langevin, the Nobel committee began to question its own award of the prize to Curie. Svante Arrhenius, a Swedish Academy member who had been an enthusiastic supporter of Curie, wrote a letter to Marie just six days after the duel and shortly after the publication of the Curie/Langevin correspondence: 'If the Academy had believed that the letter in question might be authentic, it would not, in all probability, have given you the prize before you had given a plausible explanation that the letter is false . . . I therefore hope that you will telegraph M Aurivillius or even me that it is impossible to come [to Sweden to receive the prize] . . . and that you will then write a letter saying that you do not want to accept the prize before the Langevin trial has demonstrated that the accusations made towards you are absolutely without foundation.'[127]

Marie Curie was eloquent and unambiguous in her response, sent by letter, not telegram. *The action which you advise would appear to be a grave error on my part. In fact the prize has been awarded for the discovery of Radium and Polonium. I believe that there is no connection between my scientific work and the facts of private life . . . I cannot accept the idea in principle that the appreciation of the value of scientific work should be influenced by libel and slander concerning private life. I am convinced that this opinion is shared by many people. I am very saddened that you are not yourself of this opinion.*[128] By telegram she sent her announcement to the committee in Stockholm: she would be there for the ceremonies.

'A CHEMISTRY OF THE IMPONDERABLE'

In her acceptance speech, Marie Curie carefully traced the history of her work, Pierre's work, and the work that they had done together. She emphasized that the research for which this second prize was awarded – the isolation of radium as a pure salt and its certified status as a bona fide new element based on her determination of its atomic weight – was hers alone. This work was, however, intimately connected with Pierre's, so much so that she felt justified in claiming her second prize as an 'homage to the memory of Pierre Curie'.[129]

Drawing attention to the fact that the second prize was awarded 'in recognition of her services to the advancement of chemistry', Curie took great pains to elucidate how significant her identification of radium as a chemical element had been in her own research and in subsequent work done by Rutherford and Soddy on their transmutation theory. Her work, she pointed out, was based on an innovative combination of chemistry, precision measurement, and the theory of radioactivity. Precision measurement had been the unifying mantra of 19th-century physics and chemistry. As Lord Kelvin had famously remarked, 'When you can measure what you are speaking about, and express it in numbers, you know something about it; but when you cannot measure it, when you cannot express it in numbers, your knowledge is of a meagre and unsatisfactory kind.'[130] Both Pierre, inventor of sensitive measuring devices such as the piezoelectric quartz electrometer, and Marie, an experimentalist formidably accomplished in delicate chemical processes, were deeply immersed in this ethos.

Indeed, Curie was a great experimenter. While experimental findings are normally seen as supporting theoretical discoveries, for Curie the opposite was true. Curie's insight that radioactivity was an atomic property of matter enabled her to use radioactivity from the start as a chemical marker, a guide to the isolation of more and more previously unknown elements. When Curie overcame her initial scepticism towards the Rutherford-Soddy theory of transmutation it was on the basis of new experimental evidence rather than the theory's far-ranging explanatory power. Curie pointedly underlined this fact in her 1911 acceptance speech: *This hypothesis [of atomic transmutation], which at first could only be enunciated together with other equally valid theories, has attained dominant importance and finally asserted itself in our minds owing to a body of experimental evidence which substantiated it.*[131]

By the end of 1911, Curie had been forced to admit defeat on many fronts. The triumph of the second Nobel Prize was not enough to shake off the darkness of a very difficult year. Her trip to Stockholm to receive her prize was an act of pure will. Already weakened by radiation, she had been physically and emotionally devastated by her failed candidature for the French Academy and the firestorm of controversy surrounding her affair with Langevin. She sold the house in Sceaux, where she and her daughters had enjoyed a large garden for five years, and bought a fourth-floor flat on the Quai de Bethune on the fashionable Île St-Louis within easy walking distance of the Sorbonne. She succumbed to a deep depression, receiving daily visits from her worried friends the Perrins and André Debierne. Finally, she suffered a serious kidney infection and was taken by ambulance to a private clinic.

The following years were largely taken up with recuperation. Her last notes in the laboratory notebook for 1911 were from 7 October. It would be 3 December 1912 before she took up laboratory work again. After recovering from her initial kidney infection, she had a kidney operation that left her near death. She subsequently spent time with her sister Bronia at a cottage in Brunoy outside Paris. When another relapse sent her to a sanatorium in Thonon in the Savoie mountains, Curie's friend Hertha Ayrton invited her to stay. Ayrton, a well-known British physicist, could easily identify with Curie's problems as a female scientist. Curie and her daughters spent a happy summer with Ayrton at a rented cottage in Highcliffe-on-Sea in Hampshire.

Once her health stabilized, Curie turned her mind to institutional business. She had been asked to move to Poland to run the Radium Institute that was being established there. In spite of her problems with the French establishment, Marie Curie was firm in her decision to stay in France. Plans had already been made to fund a Radium Institute in Paris that would be a joint venture between the Pasteur Institute and the University of Paris. Though she would continue to miss her family and support research in Poland, Marie Curie was by now a member of the French scientific elite, and she was not about to forsake it.

Construction on the buildings that were to consecrate the study of radium in France had begun, but Curie was impatient. She pestered the carpenters and came every week to meet with the architect Henri-Paul Nénot, the same architect who had built the new Sorbonne buildings nearly 20 years earlier. Pierre had died without a laboratory of his own. The Radium Institute would be an important boost to radioactivity research, but it would also provide a public memorial that would outlast any newspaper article.

War · 1914–1918

The construction of the new Radium Institute, delayed by a wet winter in 1913/14, had been achingly slow for Marie. The Sorbonne, which had earlier been ready to send Curie back to Poland, now realized the value of keeping the double Nobel laureate in its fold. It contributed the 400,000 francs it would take to build a world-class laboratory. By July 1914, two years after the initial agreement had been made, the Radium Institute was finally ready. The laboratory complex sat on rue Pierre Curie, just a few blocks from the EPCI. Twin laboratories faced each other across a small courtyard

The Radium Institute, headed by Marie Curie and funded with 400,000 francs from the Sorbonne

garden, planted on Curie's direction with plane and lime trees. (Marie had added a salaried gardener to the Institute's budget.) One laboratory would be dedicated to biological and medical research on radium and radioactivity, to be run by physician Claude Regaud and funded by the Pasteur Institute. Curie would guide the Institute from the other laboratory, a long-awaited purpose-built space staffed by dozens of workers dedicated to researching the physical and chemical nature of radiation.

But laboratory work would have to wait. In August 1914 all able-bodied young men, scientific researchers included, were mobilized to protect France from the advance of the German troops that had already broached its eastern borders. *Paris is calm*, Marie wrote to her daughters, who were holidaying at l'Arcouest with a governess, *and gives a good impression, in spite of the grief of the farewells.* In addition to worrying over the safety of her children and herself, Curie had her father and siblings in Poland on her mind. *Poland is partly occupied by the Germans. What will be left of it after their passage? I know nothing about my family.*[132]

Eve, aged ten, was largely unaware of events around her. Irène, at 17, was very much involved, emotionally and intellectually. She wrote her mother almost daily letters, reporting on events nearby, sharing her studies, and beseeching her Mé over and over to help her find a way to 'make herself useful'. Just one day after mobilization, she wrote, 'I know it's not sensible, but my own desire is to return. I daren't tell anybody that here, since everybody will say that it's silly and that I'd only serve to hinder, and yet I don't know what would become of me if I was here for the whole of the war.'[133]

Marie chose to stay in Paris despite the flurry of farewells and the approaching German troops. By 28 August, she faced the possibility of a siege of Paris, which would cut off communication. *If that should happen, endure it with courage*, she urged Irène, *for our personal*

*desires are nothing in comparison with the great struggle that is now under-
way. You must feel responsible for your sister and take care of her if we should
be separated for a longer time than I expected.*[134]

Curie's first response to a possible German attack on Paris was to take her hard-won gram of radium to Bordeaux for safe-keeping. Despite her fame she made the trip alone. Together with its shield of 20 kilograms of lead, the radium was so heavy that she could not carry it herself. On arrival in Bordeaux, she waited helplessly in the busy station square with her package – worth about a million francs – at her feet. Taxis, hotel rooms, and porters were all rarer than radium in Bordeaux at that moment. Luck arrived in the form of a friendly ministry employee who helped her secure a room for herself and her radium in a private apartment. The next morning she deposited the radium in a bank and promptly returned to Paris by military train, to the surprise of travellers who were fleeing that city.

With her children safe in Brittany, her radium safe in Bordeaux, and her new laboratory empty but for an elderly assistant with heart troubles, Marie Curie organized her own personal battle plan. She gave money to charities – for Polish aid, for national aid, for soldiers, for shelters for the poor. She bought yarn and knitted for the soldiers. She invested the money from her second Nobel Prize in French war bonds (which quickly devalued) and attempted to have the medals themselves melted down (indignant French officials refused). Having exhausted these contributions, Curie turned to more public kinds of service.

'ADVISED OF A PRESSING NEED'

Curie perceived a radiological need where military and health personnel did not. Putting aside radium, she saw that X-rays would be the most practical use of radiation in the field of war. X-rays could help doctors to quickly identify shrapnel and bullets and, when used with a special radiological screen, they could actually be employed

Unlike some intellectuals of the time, Marie Curie did not feel that all participants in World War One were equally responsible. When, in the spring of 1919, she was asked to sign an anti-war declaration, she refused on the grounds that agreement within the group would be illusory. *The difficulty I have with the form of your appeal is that it does not require the signers to be in agreement on certain elementary principles of international and social justice.*[135] Some years later, Curie found herself on the other side of the fence, as she tried unsuccessfully to convince Albert Einstein to serve as a representative for Germany on the newly formed League of Nations' Commission on Intellectual Cooperation. Shocked by the assassination of Jewish industrialist Walter Rathenau in 1922, Einstein turned down the position, fearing for his personal safety in an increasingly anti-Semitic Germany. Curie had come a long way from her early days as a 'disinterested' Polish positivist. Her developing vision of her own role as a scientist in wider culture included active advocacy on subjects of moral and political importance. Through her work on the League of Nations' international committee, she had become an international policy-maker and alliance-builder.

during surgery, guiding a doctor's scalpel directly to a foreign body. Though the amazed public and the most advanced doctors had enthusiastically embraced the new technology, X-rays had not yet come into common use. More conservative doctors were uncomfortable with the new equipment, and the rich patients who could afford the new technology were less likely to suffer the sorts of bodily injuries for which X-rays were best suited. War, on the other hand, meant wounds beyond all experience. More than half of the nearly 8.5 million French soldiers mobilized during the war would be wounded in battle.

The French army's health service was, by Curie's lights, alarmingly deficient in its use of X-rays to limit unnecessary amputation, speed diagnosis, and aid surgery. Curie was breathtakingly quick in moving from her identification of a need towards concrete action. Within ten days of troops being mobilized, she had a document from the Minister of War authorizing her to organize radiological workers in her new role as Director of the Red Cross Radiology Service.

She spent the month of September doing what she had done so

French ambulance fitted with X-ray equipment. Curie spent most of the war building up (and serving in) a fleet of X-ray ambulances, dubbed 'petites Curie' (little Curies), for the French army. She acquired her own driver's license so she could travel as quickly as possible to the battlegrounds

ably at the start of her doctoral work: gathering the materials that she would need for the task ahead. Back in 1897, this had meant mineralogical samples and precision instrumentation. Now in 1914 she needed X-ray equipment, money, and – what would prove crucial to her radiology service – automobiles donated by wealthy patrons, many of them women.

Initially she focused on serving the area around Paris. The first Battle of the Marne was fought in early September in the fields between Paris and Verdun, close enough to the city that Paris taxicabs were commandeered to bring reinforcements to the battle. It made sense at first to focus on equipping local hospitals with radiological equipment. But Curie quickly saw that X-rays in hospitals would not be enough. She would need a way to get the equipment to the wounded. At this time automobiles were far outnumbered by the hundreds of thousands of horses that still served to transport and supply the French army. But Marie realized that, in addition to delivering X-ray apparatus to where it was needed most, X-ray units in cars could generate their own electricity. The electrical current needed to power the X-ray apparatus was often otherwise unattainable in the field hospitals at the front.

By September, the Germans had been pushed back from Paris, and it was safe for Irène and Eve to return. Both went back to study, Eve to school and Irène to a crash-course in nursing. Marie continued raising funds and gathering equipment with which to fit out her first radiological car. *It was simply a touring motor-car, arranged for the transport of a complete radiological apparatus, together with a dynamo that was worked by the engine of the car, and furnished the electric current necessary for the production of the rays.*[136]

Curie later wrote a book on the experience, titled *Radiology and War*, which outlined both the scientific and the practical knowledge necessary for using X-rays in wartime. It reads like a how-to guide, and in spite of the horrifying nature of the casualties, one senses Marie Curie's intense satisfaction in a job well done. *Advised of a pressing need,* she wrote, *the radiology car departs . . . carrying all its supplies and its provision of gasoline. That doesn't prevent it from moving at the speed of 25 miles an hour when the state of the road permits it. The personnel consist of a doctor, a technician and a chauffeur, but on a good team each transcends his métier.*[137]

Arriving at the field hospitals, the team set about creating a temporary treatment room, blacking out the windows, setting up the X-ray apparatus, and creating an improvised dark-room in under an hour. First the chauffeur laid the cable connecting the dynamo in the car to the X-ray equipment. Then the surgeon and Curie would work together in the darkened room. She would regulate the apparatus so that the doctor could clearly distinguish bone, muscle, and any foreign objects. Occasionally the doctor would operate immediately, following his work on the radiographic screen. More often, notes and photographs would be taken, and the patient operated on later.

With just a month of formal training under her belt, Irène joined her mother, witnessing the horrific injuries caused by German machine guns, mortar fire, and bombs. Irène was mature beyond her years and had inherited her mother's steely will. By September 1915, aged 18, she was working alone as a radiological nurse in army hospitals. Her letters record her excitement and toughness, as well as her disdain for those who were less competent than she. Of a witless surgeon who did not respond to her lessons in the calculations needed to locate shrapnel, she wrote, 'I truly believe he does not know any geometry; he can't even make the calculations for the displacement method with assurance.'[138]

Once she had a few mobile units up and running, Marie realized many more were needed. Approaching wealthy women such as the Marquise de Ganay and the Princess Murat, she asked them to donate their limousines to the war effort. She successfully convinced both the wealthy and the bureaucrats to support her endeavour. By her own count, she established some 200 radiological stations, and equipped 20 cars in her laboratory in the first two years of the war. She also learned to drive, learned enough mechanics to keep the cars functioning on the very bumpy wartime roads, and kept a flat-nosed Renault for herself, so that she could take off at a moment's notice.

Her sense of urgency was great. In four years, she visited over 300 hospitals in France and Belgium, at Amiens, Ypres, Verdun, Reims, Calais, Poperinghe, and other battle sites. *I have had a letter saying that the radiological car working in the Saint-Pol region has been damaged,* she wrote to Paul Langevin. *This means that the whole area is without any radiological service! I am taking the necessary steps to hasten my departure and am resolved to put all my strength at the service of my adopted country, since I cannot do anything for my unfortunate native country*

From 1919 Irène assisted her mother at the Radium Institute. In this photograph, taken in 1921, the two women are using a piezoelectric quartz electrometer

just now, bathed as it is in blood after more than a century of suffering.[139]

As the numbers of the mobile X-ray cars, dubbed 'petites Curie', rose, more people needed to be trained to operate them. Curie used her otherwise idle Radium Institute to set up a school to train young women and men in the X-ray techniques needed in wartime. From 1915 until the war ended, she taught 150 students lessons on electricity, X-rays, and anatomy, and gave them practical exercises in using X-ray equipment. They were then sent to serve in wartime radiological posts.

Despite her admirable speed in recognizing the benefits of X-rays, Curie was still reluctant to admit, or even investigate, the harmful effects that accompanied their use. Marie complained at one point that a woman had tried to leave her course *because of the harmful effect of rays*[140] The protective measures that she employed against X-rays were, like those she used with radium, quite primitive. A small metal screen, cloth gloves and smocks, and a reminder to stay out of the direct path of the X-ray beam were the extent of the precautions. Curie's lackadaisical attitude toward radiation-related injuries lasted her whole life. While the novelty of the technology and the lack of data on injuries can explain some of her reluctance, Curie had witnessed more incidences of deleterious radium exposure than most. She of all people was well placed to recognize the harmful effects.

Despite her own overexposure to X-rays, Irène was thriving in the intense and demanding environment of war. Alongside her radiological work in the field and the help she gave her mother with training at the Radium Institute, Irène continued her own studies. 'I am sending you my calculations for the equalization of kinetic energies,' she wrote to her mother in August 1917. 'It is very easy, but the other time I made a small error in the "discussion". I redid the calculation for pressure and for the case where the distribution of speed is unknown . . . I eat well and I sleep like a marmot.'[141]

Between 1915 and 1917 Irène earned three separate degrees with distinction at the Sorbonne, in mathematics, physics, and chemistry.

Marie Curie's mind was never far from her first scientific love. Within a year, she had retrieved her gram of radium from the Bordeaux safe-deposit box and was supplying the emanations from it (what we now call radon gas) to civil and military hospitals. Naturally emitted by decaying radium, this gas was collected and sealed in glass tubes by workers at the Radium Institute. Doctors used the radiation from the tubes to treat tumours and skin lesions, with somewhat lacklustre results.

SCIENTIFIC CONQUESTS

The radiological units that Curie established, both fixed and mobile, carried out some one million wartime examinations in all. It was a remarkable achievement. But what impact did the war have on Curie? Her published writings are taciturn. She saw it as her duty to serve, not to suffer. A paragraph in the autobiographical notes included in her biography of Pierre conveys some of the emotions she experienced while working in the radiological outposts. *To hate the very idea of war, it ought to be sufficient to see once what I have seen so many times, all over these years: men and boys brought to the advanced ambulance in a mixture of mud and blood, many of them dying of their injuries and many others recovering but slowly, in the space of months, with pain and suffering.*[142]

But, even though war had destroyed millions of lives and greatly affected Curie's own life, she was careful to reflect on the possible benefits of the conflict for the budding science of radiation. *The story of radiology in war offers a striking example of the unsuspected amplitude that the application of purely scientific discoveries can take under certain conditions,* she wrote in her book *Radiology and War. What had seemed difficult became easy and received an immediate solution.* During the war, X-rays and medical radium therapy, both of which had languished in the half-light of notoriety and novelty, came into their own. *The scientific discovery achieved the conquest of its natural field of action.*[143]

Curie was aware of the terrible contrast between wartime suffering and loss of life and the scientific conquest she so celebrated. But rather than exploring further the links between science and society, she reiterated her familiar creed of the nobly detached scientist – a figure increasingly remote from the reality of her own situation. *What are we to conclude from these unhoped-for developments revealed to us by science at the end of the 19th century? It seems that they must make our confidence in disinterested research more alive and increase our reverence and admiration for it.*[144] While Curie felt gratified, to say the least, by her successful scientific innovations in wartime medicine, she was notably silent on the German use of poison gas.

From the start Marie Curie had advocated a peculiar brand of scientific detachment and disinterest that could be both dogmatic and surprisingly flexible. She and Pierre had categorically refused to patent their discoveries, even though funds from patents would have helped finance further research and discovery. Yet they had enjoyed sustained, mutually beneficial relationships with industrial producers of radium. Curie was dedicated to a higher cause and was part of a community of disinterested researchers. But at the same time, she perceived herself as powerless – and thus licensed to make alliances where she could. She felt powerless because the state still had to be convinced – to a degree difficult to imagine now – of the value of scientific expertise and the need for scientific funding. Curie's battles with the establishment, her years without a proper laboratory or academic job, the prejudice against her as a woman and a Pole, even her experiences with reluctant French officials at the start of the war had made her, in spite of herself, into a political animal.

Final Years · 1919–1934

Marie Curie had grown adept at putting off the endless stream of admirers, suppliants, and journalists seeking a new angle on a well-worn story. But in May 1920 a petite American with a taste for fashionable hats, and a persistence to match Curie's own, made it through the bulwarks. Marie Mattingly Meloney, Missy to her friends, was an intelligent, well-to-do, and influential woman. An editor for *The Delineator*, a popular American women's magazine, she was in Europe on a visiting tour that included meetings with H G Wells, J M Barrie, and Bertrand Russell. She was, like Curie, a woman who had achieved startling success in a man's world, as Washington Bureau Chief for the *Denver Post* and the editor of a well-respected magazine at just 39.

An unabashed Curie enthusiast, she had come to spend a few moments with the woman who had 'been important to me for 20 years'. A curious thing must have happened in the interview. The two women, both outwardly frail and inwardly tenacious, enjoyed each other's company. Though she was visiting simply as a fan, eager no doubt for some new copy for her magazine, Meloney left with a new sense of purpose.

Marie, as shrewd as ever, had been quick to tell Meloney how sorely her laboratory lacked radium. In 1920 there were an estimated 140 grams of purified radium in the world.[145] Fifty of those grams were stored across America; France had just one. This gram, the core of Curie's laboratory, was the product of decades of work on her part. She could not afford to buy more and she could not hope to create more herself.

This was a challenge Missy Meloney could embrace. Her cable address was 'Idealism' and her contacts extended all the way to the White House, where vice-president Calvin Coolidge was a friend. Rather than simply selling Marie Curie to her readers for the price of a magazine, she would use the platform of her editorship to make them reach deeper into their pockets. She would raise enough money from the women of America to buy another gram of radium for Curie's laboratory. The cost? $100,000 – nearly a million of today's dollars.

Meloney's campaign has all the hallmarks of a modern publicity barrage. Book deal tie-ins were negotiated (Curie published an autobiography, at Meloney's behest, to coincide with the fund-raising), and advice proffered: 'You may receive letters from Macmillan publishing house, Scribner's, Dutton and Houghton Mifflin. These four houses are among the best American publishing companies. I am suggesting they make definite offers to you. For your own information: the fairest proposition would probably be an advance of a thousand dollars and a royalty . . . Twenty per cent was about the rate given Theodore Roosevelt, and is a really very fine contract.'[146] Scientific and fund-raising advisory committees were formed to which Mrs John D Rockefeller, Mrs Calvin Coolidge, and representatives from Harvard, Cornell, and Columbia Universities, and

Marie Mattingly Meloney, American editor and fundraiser *par excellence*

the American Medical Association all lent their names and influence. The star attraction of the campaign was Curie herself, who was to charm and impress America on a whirlwind tour.

Never having left Europe and understandably unnerved by high-profile press coverage that must have recalled for her the scandals of 1911, Curie was reluctant. Some of Meloney's cables had casually referred to one grain of radium. Curie cabled back, through a friend, to clarify: 'Madame Curie asked if one grain or gram. Grain insufficient justify absence here, being one fifteenth of a gram.'[147]

Had she said grain? Of course Meloney meant gram. Curie was careful to ask what the legal status of the donated radium would be. Would the University of Paris have any claims on it? Meloney wrote back promptly. 'The gram of radium is for you, *for your own personal use* and to be disposed of by you after your death. I shall be glad to be of use to the University of Paris if it needs assistance, but for the present my time and energies are concerned only with your personal interests.'[148]

Curie's health continued to deteriorate. Her ears buzzed and her cataracts prevented her from seeing clearly at the Paris Opera gala that was organized for her send-off in late April 1920. The great actress Sarah Bernhardt read out 'An Ode to Madame Curie' at the gala: 'No, you have never led an army, / No voices whispered stern commands. / But your sincere consuming ardour / Far outshines the burning brands.'[149] Lest they lose her to America, the French made it clear: no longer 'that Polish woman', Curie was once again a national treasure.

She arrived in America to find Missy's publicity machine humming. A special Marie Curie issue of *The Delineator* was on sale at newsstands. 'That Millions Shall Not Die!' was the headline, setting the tone for a campaign that would inflate precarious hopes for curing cancer with radium. Radiotherapy, or Curietherapy as it became known in France, was still a young and inexact branch of medicine. Nonetheless, an editorial in *The Delineator* gushed that 'The foremost American scientists say that Madame Curie, provided with a single gram of radium, may advance science to the point where cancer to a very large extent may be eliminated.'[150] Curie herself intended to use the gram for pure research and had told Meloney as much. But Curie was certainly interested in the medical

Unlike X-rays, which were used in diagnosis and treatment almost immediately following their discovery, radium, being both expensive and rare, was incorporated into medicine more slowly. Nevertheless, by the end of World War One doctors were using the wonder element to treat cancer, gout, a form of tuberculosis of the skin, arthritis, dermatitis, and a host of more general complaints. Though doctors understood that too much radiation could cause painful burns and in extreme cases even death, early treatment protocols were based on scant data and success rates were low. For most treatments, a small glass ampoule filled with radium or radon gas was placed near the diseased tissue; it was hoped the radiation would kill unhealthy cancerous cells and slow tumour growth. Patients were also advised to drink water that had been 'fortified' by being stored in a radioactive container.

The well-publicized and gruesome death of American Eben Byers in 1932 changed all that. On his doctor's advice, playboy millionaire Byers had been drinking radioactive water marketed under the brand Radiothor as a treatment for fatigue, muscle aches, and joint pain. He drank several bottles a day for nearly five years before succumbing to a set of mysterious symptoms, including severe disintegration of his jaw and teeth and extreme weight loss, which rapidly worsened until he died at the age of 52 weighing just 92 pounds (42 kilograms). After his death, regulations were introduced that sharply limited the use of radioactivity in consumer products. Today, radioactive elements and radiation are still used to treat cancers. By focusing the beams of an X-ray machine or placing a small amount of a radioactive element near a tumour, doctors use radiation to kill diseased cells while attempting to limit damage to the surrounding healthy tissue. Strict safety standards protect doctors against overexposure and patients are warned of the (slight) risks from radiation. Though Curie is often seen as a pioneer in using radium to treat cancer, she did not have any medical training and her only direct contribution to medicine was her work with X-rays during the war.

uses of radium and this was enough for Meloney, who knew that donors responded better to miracle cures than esoteric physics.

A barrage of feature articles in other publications ranging from the *Kansas City Post* to the *New York Evening World* spun variations on the now-established Curie myth of persistence and deprivation. These headlines capture another aspect of the legend: Curie's all too apparent frailty. The 'simple charm of tired visitor' hints at the exhaustion another reporter was less delicate in describing. 'Her thin shoulders are bent with much stooping over laboratory tables, the hair, brushed back uncompromisingly from her lined forehead, is snow white; there is nothing young about the sharpened contour of her chin, jaw and throat.'[151] Marie Curie was 54, hardly an old woman, but her body betrayed the damaging effects of radiation.

Curie visiting Columbia University, New York, 1921

Curie made it through a month of appearances at colleges, museums, and lecture halls across the east coast. On 20 May, she received from President Harding the gift she had come for: a token of the gram of radium that had been purchased for her with the proceeds of Meloney's campaign (the real thing having been safely left in the factory until her departure). In the photographs she is beaming with delight, but she was close to exhaustion. She managed to carry out a few more official duties – the opening of the low-temperature Laboratory of Mines in Washington, a tour of the massive radium factory in Pittsburgh, the acceptance of a medal from the American Philosophical Society (she gave them a piezoelectric quartz electrometer in return) – before abandoning her schedule due to the stress of, as one paper put it, 'Too Much Hospitality'.[152]

By late June, after a few weeks free from public appearances, Marie was ready to visit the laboratories of a few east coast universities, including that of Bertram Boltwood, the Yale physicist who had opposed her radium standard some ten years previously. Boltwood was no friend of Curie's, referring to her in an earlier letter

Curie with US President Warren Harding

to Rutherford as a 'a plain darn fool',[153] and had gone so far as to attempt to withdraw from a welcoming committee organized by the American Chemical Society.

In the event, Boltwood was 'quite pleasantly surprised to find that she was quite keen about scientific matters and in an unusually amiable mood', despite her obviously weakened condition. But he was not above sniping to Rutherford that 'she certainly made a good clean-up over here and took back a gram of radium and quite a tidy number of thousands of dollars.' Boltwood hid any envy he may have felt of Curie's fund-raising coup by choosing to pity her instead. 'I felt sorry for the poor old girl. She was a distinctly pathetic figure. She was very modest and unassuming, and she seemed frightened at all the fuss the people made over her.'[154]

America had indeed made a fuss of Curie, to the tune of over $150,000. In addition to the money needed to purchase the gram of radium, which accompanied Curie home on the *Olympic*, Meloney's campaign had generated a further $50,000 to be spent on research and materials.

The Marie Curie who returned from this first trip to America (there would be another, in eight years, to raise money for an additional gram of radium to be used in her beloved Poland) was a woman of international fame and impressive institutional power. Marie Curie would never again cower in fear of the next day's newspapers. She would spend the rest of her life consolidating the empire of radium that she had worked hard to create. In the period following her trip to America, Curie travelled with the zeal of the newly converted. She tended to combine attendance at a scientific conference with travel to destinations with charms of their own – Rio de Janeiro, Italy, Holland, Spain, a cruise across the South Atlantic.

While Curie began to explore a world away from the laboratories and factories, hospitals and mines that had been the principal destinations of her working life, she also broadened her personal commitments. Having formerly avoided any non-scientific appointments, in 1922 she decided to serve on the newly formed League of Nations' International Commission on Intellectual Cooperation. *I believe international work is a heavy task, but that it is nevertheless indispensable to go through an apprenticeship in it, at the cost of many efforts and a real spirit of sacrifice: however imperfect it may be, the work of Geneva has a grandeur which deserves support.*[155] While she had not sought the nomination, she accepted it and was to serve for 12 years, working to establish shared resources for international science, such as bibliographies, scholarships, and rules for safeguarding individuals' discoveries. If this last item seems strange for a woman whose life had been shaped by her refusal to patent her work, Curie had at least always been careful to clarify exactly what achievements she should receive credit for.

World War One had brought to fruition one of Curie's childhood dreams: the creation of an independent Polish republic. Poland's liberation from Russian domination in 1920 ended 123 years of foreign rule. Polish soldiers had fought in three armies during the war, under Russian, German, and Austrian leadership, each promising them autonomy after the war. In the end, a Pole, Marshal Piłsudski entered Warsaw and took it for himself and his fellow Poles.

Marie Curie had left Poland at the age of 24. Though she had returned often, and still more frequently yearned for it, she had chosen, willingly and repeatedly, to stay in France. As a young woman with uncertain prospects, she had returned to Paris to marry Pierre and to continue her studies when she might have become a teacher in Warsaw instead. As a mature scientist subject to the indifference (sometimes hostility) of the French establishment and the occasional calumny of the French press, she had resisted good offers to establish herself in Poland. Marie Curie could never return to being Manya Skłodowska.

But Curie's nostalgia for friends and family, and the stronger force of a duty to serve her country had never left her. On learning of Poland's long-awaited independence, she quoted the Polish exile poet Mickiewicz to her brother *So now we, 'born in servitude and chained since birth', we have seen that resurrection of our country which has been our dream. We did not hope to live until this moment ourselves; we thought it might not even be given to our children to see it – and it is here!*[156]

Despite the success of her fund-raising trip to America and her work for the League of Nations, Curie was in some respects leading a significantly diminished life. Her eyes were now so weak that she had resorted to writing her lecture notes in huge letters and pasting coloured signs on her instruments. She would eventually undergo four operations to treat her cataracts. Reluctant to admit that radium might be the cause, she kept the surgery secret from all but her family members. To her sister Bronia she confided: *My greatest troubles come from my eyes and ears. My eyes have grown much weaker, and probably very little can be done about them. As for the ears, an almost continuous humming, sometimes very intense, persecutes me. I am very worried about it: my work may be interfered with – or even become impossible. Perhaps radium has something to do with these troubles, but it cannot be affirmed with certainty.*[157]

The war had exposed millions to X-rays and seen the introduction of radium emanations for the treatment of skin lesions and cancers. As more patients were treated, more doctors and technicians were exposed to radiation. They reported symptoms ranging from irritations of the skin, referred to as radiodermatitis, to severe radium necrosis (tissue death), which could lead to gangrene and death. Evidence that scientific workers were at risk was also mounting. Madame Artaud, a member of the Radiochemistry Society and an acquaintance of Curie, died not long after spilling a highly radioactive substance on herself. Within four days of each other in 1925, the engineers Maurice Deminitroux and Marcel Demalander died of leukaemia and severe anaemia after being exposed some months earlier while preparing radioactive substances for medical use at a factory outside Paris. Newspaper articles depicting the dead as martyrs to radium fed a growing awareness of the dangers of radioactivity. The first radiation protection committee began to meet in Britain in 1921 to work out detailed recommendations to safeguard workers from X-rays and radium. The risks to patients were not yet considered significant.

In America, where the radium industry was booming, young women worked as dial-painters in factories where they used fine-tipped brushes to paint numbers on to wristwatches and instrument dials with luminous radium. Workers at the US Radium Company, in Orange, New Jersey, followed the custom of shaping the end of the brush to a sharp point with their lips, ingesting quantities of radium with every lick. Radium was damaging enough when outside the body. Once ingested, radium, which is chemically similar to calcium, is deposited in the bones. From there it causes anaemia, weakened bones, and cancer of the bone and marrow. Dozens of young women dial-painters suffered painful deaths, their jaws disfigured by necrosis and their bodies overrun by tumours. Both government agencies and the companies involved responded slowly to the reality of radium poisoning, a new industrial disease they were neither ready nor willing to recognize. It would not be until 1928, when 15 young women had already died, that the International X-ray and Radium Protection Committee was established at the Second International Congress of Radiology.

Marie Curie had always encouraged an atmosphere of tough-minded endurance in her laboratory. Radiation burns were badges of honour to be worn with pride. Curie's own radiation-burned fingers attest to the damage she sustained. Pierre, who had done early experiments on the effects of radium on himself and on guinea pigs, had been sanguine about radiation damage. 'In fact, I am happy after all with my injury. My wife is as pleased as I,' he told a reporter back in 1903. 'You see, these are the little accidents of the laboratory: they shouldn't frighten people who live their lives among alembics and retorts.'[158] Not all were so happy with their injuries. Sonia Cotelle, a long-time worker in the measurements service of the Curie laboratory, had an accident in which polonium exploded in her face. Irène wrote to her mother that Cotelle was 'in very bad health . . . she has stomach troubles, an extremely rapid loss of hair, etc.', but was quick to add that since she herself had 'worked a lot on that without being made ill, I think more that she must have swallowed some polonium as the activity of her lips would lead one to think and her urine. What's more her present ill health perhaps has no connection with that but she is very uneasy, which is understandable.'[159]

Despite the Curies' cavalier attitude towards the dangers of

Marie on the balcony of the Radium Institute. Radiation burns are visible on her fingers

radium, Curie followed contemporary safety practices in her laboratory. By 1921, Curie's lab workers had routine blood tests to monitor anaemia, as radium was known to damage red blood cells. Researchers used hoods to extract radium emanations from the laboratory, sources of radioactivity were encased in lead, and when researchers worked with radioactive materials they did so behind a protective lead screen (at least one inch thick) and held tubes with forceps, not fingers.

In response to a 1925 report that stressed the dangers inherent in the industrial preparation of radioactive material, Curie commented that *it was necessary to warn of danger, to industrialists as well as to engineers* but that she was unaware of any *grave accidents due to radium or to mesothorium among the personnel of other factories . . . [nor] among the personnel of my Institute.*[160] But by 1931 seven out of 20 workers at the Radium Institute showed anomalies in their blood tests. Curie would only occasionally admit, as she had when her strength had failed on her first trip to America, that radioactivity was the cause of her own failing eyesight and weakened constitution.

TWO DAUGHTERS

During this time, Marie depended on her daughters as she never had before. The two had grown into remarkably different young women, each self-possessed, both in awe of their mother. They divided their care of Marie along tacit but entrenched lines. Eve, now 18, tended to Marie at home, acting as a combination wife, nurse, and cook in their large but awkwardly furnished flat on Île St-Louis. Irène accompanied her mother to work at the Radium Institute. In the evenings, the two scientists analysed the work of the day, leaving Eve to imagine the meaning of the algebraic terms they discussed. What did BB (pronounced like *bébé*, the French word for baby) 'prime' and Bb² mean? 'These unknown "babies" of whom Marie and Irène Curie were for ever talking must be charming, Eve thought . . . But why *square* babies? And *prime* babies? What were their privileges?'[161]

Eve had not grown into a scientific companion for her mother. She had been an empathetic child, musically gifted and attuned to the emotional life of others. Her mother had encouraged Eve's energetic pursuit of a career as a concert pianist, buying her a grand piano and paying for her lessons. One day she arranged for the great pianist and fellow Pole Ignacy Jan Paderewski to listen to Eve's playing. *Paderewski thinks that she has exceptional ability,* she recorded proudly in her notebook. *I had an intuition about it, I who understand nothing of music, I felt very much that she didn't play like just anyone . . . When I heard her play 'Marlborough', I always said to myself, 'A child doesn't play like that.'*[162]

In addition to her musical interests, Eve tried playwriting, criticism, and journalism. She was a fashionable young woman whose mother did not always understand her. *Oh my poor darling!* Eve remembers her mother exclaiming, as she watched her daughter dress for an evening. *What dreadful heels! No, you'll never make me believe that women were made to walk on stilts . . . And what sort of new style is this, to have the back of the dress cut out? Décolletage in front was bearable, just; but these miles and miles of naked back! First of all, it's indecent; secondly, it makes you run the risk of pleurisy; thirdly, it is ugly: the third argument ought to touch you if the others don't.*[163]

Despite Curie's support for Eve's musical abilities, the bond between Irène and her mother was more intimate. *We will have to reconcile the scientific work represented by us two with the musical art represented by Evette,* Marie wrote to Irène. In this period, Irène grew into the role of heiress-apparent to her mother's scientific kingdom. Irène's interest in science and her single-minded drive had manifested themselves even before the critical experience of working alongside her mother during the war had jump-started her precocious career. She had also inherited her mother's lack of interest in fashion and social niceties, wearing dowdy shoes and black stockings and often communicating with a brusqueness that bordered on rudeness. In 1925, at a party held to celebrate her presentation of her doctoral thesis on the alpha rays of polonium, the tea was served in the laboratory glassware and little cakes were laid out on the photography trays.

Frédéric Joliot-Curie

Irène had not inherited her mother's shyness, but she had fully imbibed the spirit of high-minded sacrifice that had shaped Marie's life. 'A woman of science should renounce worldly obligations', she told the reporter who had been sent to cover her graduation.[164] Luckily for Irène, she had found, like her mother, a companion for work and love. Irène had met Frédéric Joliot in her mother's laboratory while teaching him radioactive techniques. Slightly younger than Irène at 25 years old, Joliot had an excellent scientific pedigree, having graduated first in his class from the EPCI under the watchful eye of Pierre's successor Paul Langevin. He and Irène were married two years after their first meeting. Marie would overcome initial misgivings to come to see Frédéric as a *ball of fire* with whom she frequently engaged in rapid scientific discussions.

In 1923 the French government awarded Curie a lifetime annual pension of 40,000 francs. She spent her savings on property in the holiday locations she had been visiting for 20 years. She bought a house in the warmth of the Mediterranean coast, in a place called Cavalaire, where she often travelled in the winters. She also built a white-plastered house on the moor above the sea at l'Arcouest, a small village on the Brittany coast that was a seasonal home to a group of Sorbonne intellectuals who dubbed it 'Port Science'. Headed by historian Charles Seignobos, the group included the physicists Jean Perrin, André Debierne, and Victor Auger, the mathematician Emile Borel, and the biologists Louis Lapique and Charles Maurain. For years Curie had taken holidays in this rarefied community, improving her ranking in the jargon of the group from an undignified 'elephant' to a sea-worthy 'sailor' by summers spent sailing and swimming.[165] Despite, or perhaps because of, her physical ailments, she swam in the ocean with an almost childlike joy. 'The picture of Marie Curie swimming at Roch Vras in that cool deep water of ideal purity and transparence is one of the most delightful memories I have of my mother,' wrote Eve, who was a child during these early holidays. 'Methodically trained by Irène

The Sorbonne intellectuals on holiday at l'Arcouest, 'Port Science'

and Eve, she had learned an overarm stroke in good style. Her innate elegance and grace had done the rest. You forgot her grey hair, hidden under the bathing cap, and her wrinkled face, in admiring the slim, supple body, the pretty white arms, and the lively charming gestures of a young girl.'[166]

SCIENTIFIC SPAWN

Though Curie spent a great deal of time away from the laboratory in the years following the war, she kept an active hand in the work of the Radium Institute, which grew from employing a handful of workers immediately after the war to between 30 and 40 by 1930. She continued her lectures at the Sorbonne and kept up friendships with Jean Perrin and Missy Meloney, with whom she exchanged regular letters.

Curie treated her researchers well but she kept her distance. 'She does not appear to come around much to the students but receives them very kindly when they seek her,' commented May Sybil Leslie, a researcher who had won an 1851 Exhibition Scholarship to fund her stay at the Curie laboratory.[167] Occasionally, this famous reserve would break, and Curie would laugh or tease. Several of her workers described such moments in their later memoirs, suggesting that they were lapses worth remembering. Some 40 years after her first meeting with Curie, Hélène Emmanuel-Zavizziano would recall how 'This woman, pale and thin in a narrow black dress, who scrutinized me with her cold, penetrating look, paralyzed me into timidity at first. But she began to ask me questions with such great simplicity, and her face relaxed into a smile so full of charm, that I allowed myself to go ahead and tell her of my disappointments as a beginning researcher and she decided to accept me into her Radium Institute.'[168]

Did Curie pave the way for women in science? Many of the workers at the Institute were, like Curie herself, women who had left their native countries to pursue opportunities in science that were otherwise unavailable to them. They came to Paris from Sweden, Romania, Russia, America, and Poland. They struggled to find funding, to maintain relationships (many never married), and, on leaving Curie's laboratory and returning to their native countries, to create scientific careers for themselves.

Ellen Gleditsch, perhaps the most successful (apart from Irène) of any female worker at the Curie laboratory, may stand as a representative figure. Gleditsch

Marie Curie in the laboratory at the Radium Institute

spent five years with Curie, between 1907 and 1912, working on technical as well as theoretical problems in radioactivity. She became a close personal friend of Curie and helped locate

WOMEN IN SCIENCE

radium-containing minerals on her summer holidays in Norway. After her time in Paris, she struggled to find further scientific work. She was granted a modest fellowship at the University of Oslo where she complained about the lack of equipment. She later went to Yale on a year-long scholarship from the American-Scandinavian foundation. While there she managed eventually to convince the chauvinistic Boltwood of her considerable scientific acumen.

In spite of Curie's achievements, Gleditsch still had to fight to gain access to laboratories as a female scientist. Unlike Curie, who entered the scientific community alongside her husband, and tasted major international success early, Gleditsch was on her own. Gleditsch – like many other women in science – also found it difficult to reconcile the demands of traditional marriage with the stimulating and arduous life of the laboratory.

Curie was perhaps herself ambivalent about the role of women in science. Some of her writing suggests that she viewed her life as exceptional, neither a desirable nor feasible option for most other women. *It isn't necessary to lead such an anti-natural existence as mine. I have given a great deal of time to science because I wanted to, because I loved research . . . What I want for women and young girls is a simple family life and some work that will interest them.*[169]

Despite her (continuing) importance as an icon for female scientists, Curie considered the institutions she created to be her more significant legacy. By 1930 the cluster of buildings of the Radium Institute had grown to a small prefecture. Curie's original laboratory had doubled in size, Regaud's medical laboratory had added an outpatient unit, and a new biological laboratory was under construction. Curie had long been the beneficiary of private funding that enabled her institute to operate independently of the university. In the 1920s she received a series of new grants from the Rothschild and Rockefeller foundations that funded two new institutes on the rue Pierre Curie, the Henri Poincaré Institute of

Mathematics and Physical Mathematics and the Institute of Physical Chemistry.

These new institutions and the relentless campaigning of Jean Perrin paved the way for a reorganization of scientific funding in France. Though it was accomplished after her death, Curie would have been proud to know that the tradition of pursuing scientific research separately from education which she had helped establish led directly to the formation of the *Centre National de la Recherche Scientifique* (National Centre for Scientific Research), or CNRS. This body, run by ambitious and energetic scientists (Marie's son-in-law Frédédic Joliot-Curie would later be a director) replaced the staid, closed ranks of the Academy of Sciences as the arbiter of new directions in French scientific research. By separating funding for education from funding for research, the CNRS was able to foster scientists working outside the academic establishment who might previously have been neglected, as Marie and Pierre had been in their early years.

Aside from overseeing the growth of this centre of independent scientific activity on the rue Pierre Curie, Marie had the satisfaction of travelling to Warsaw in 1925 to lay the cornerstone for a Radium Institute there. Her sister Bronia, acting as architect, agent, and treasurer, had raised money for the Institute with the slogan 'Buy a brick for the Marie Skłodowska-Curie Institute.' As the Institute slowly took shape, it became apparent that the stocks of radium in Poland were inadequate for the cancer treatment that was the Institute's *raison d'être*. It was on this excuse that Marie made a second trip to America. With Meloney's expert help, once again Curie was able to raise the money to buy a gram of radium. Curie had learned the art of travel and this time she seems to have genuinely enjoyed her trip. She stayed overnight at the White House as a friend of President Hoover, celebrated the golden jubilee of the electric light with Henry Ford, and attended a dinner in honour of Thomas

Edison. She left America on 26 October 1929 with enough money for a gram of radium and funds left over for the Curie Foundation. She completed her trip just in time. Three days later, the stock market crashed.

While Marie gradually retreated from a leading role in her laboratory, her daughter and son-in-law were doing the work that would earn them a Nobel Prize: the creation of artificial radioactivity by bombarding a non-radioactive substance with radioactivity. Though Marie had noticed early on radium's peculiar ability to contaminate substances with which it came into contact, it had previously been thought that radioactivity was solely a naturally occurring feature of certain elements such as uranium and radium. On 15 January 1934, the very day that Irène and Frédéric first produced artificial radioactivity, they reproduced the experiment for Marie Curie and Paul Langevin. 'I will never forget the expression of intense joy which overtook her when Irène and I showed her the first [artificially produced] radioactive element in a little glass tube,' Frédéric later wrote. 'I can see her still taking this little tube of the radioelement, already quite weak, in her radium-damaged fingers. To verify what we were telling her, she brought the Geiger-Muller counter up close to it and she could hear the numerous clicks . . . This was without a doubt the last great satisfaction of her life.' For this discovery, Irène and Frédéric would win the Nobel Prize in chemistry in 1935.

During the last few years of her life, Curie researched the actinium family, with further plans to study the 'fine structure' of the alpha rays, but she was plagued by worsening bouts of poor health. In 1932, a simple broken wrist led to a lingering convalescence and the next year X-rays revealed a large gallstone in her stomach. Her Polish family, the close-knit group she had left behind

Marie (seated on the right) and Irène with research assistants, including André Debierne (standing on the right)

Marie Curie in 1931, three years before her death

so long ago, seemed more important than ever. *I, too, am sad that we are separated,* she wrote to Bronia. *But even though you feel lonely, you have one consolation just the same: there are three of you in Warsaw, and thus you can have some company and some protection. Believe me, family solidarity is, after all, the only good thing. I have been deprived of it, so I know. Try to get some comfort out of it, and don't forget your Parisian sister: let us see each other as often as possible.*[170]

She and Bronia made one last trip together in the spring of 1934 to the house in Cavalaire, where a cold and the chill of the unheated house sent Curie into deep, despairing sobs. Despite a persistent fever, she returned to the laboratory with plans to continue her research on actinium. One sunny May afternoon that year, she left early, reminding the gardener to tend to a sick rose bush in the garden she had planted 20 years earlier. It was to be her last day of work.

Marie's health worsened rapidly. Doctors could not fix on a diagnosis, alternating between 'flu and bronchitis. Old tubercular lesions and some inflammation of the lung led them to suggest a sanatorium in Switzerland. Eve duly took her mother to the Saint-Gervais sanatorium there, where tests showed that Curie's lungs were not infected, but by then her strength was almost gone. At the end, Eve stayed with her mother alone, listening to her fragmented speech – *I've been thinking of that publication . . . Was it done with radium or with mesothorium? . . . It wasn't the medicines that made me better. It was the pure air, the altitude . . .* – and protecting her from the knowledge of her imminent death.

Marie Curie died at dawn on 4 July 1934. The official cause of death was 'aplastic pernicious anaemia of rapid, feverish development. The bone marrow did not react, probably because it had been injured by a long accumulation of radiations.' She was 67.

She was buried in a simple ceremony at Sceaux. As she had wished, her coffin was lowered into the grave on top of Pierre's. Instead of prayers, she was buried with two handfuls of Polish soil brought from Warsaw by Bronia and Józef.

In 1995, Marie and Pierre's remains were transferred in wooden coffins from the country cemetery to the domed Panthéon in Paris, just blocks from the EPCI and the Radium Institute. Marie remains the only woman to be honoured for her own achievements in France's monument to its 'great men'.

Irène and Frédéric Joliot-Curie accept the Nobel Prize for chemistry from King Gustav V of Sweden in Stockholm in 1935

Irène Joliot-Curie · 1897–1956

by Sabine Seifert

Situated behind the Panthéon, in the quiet part of Paris's Latin Quarter, is the little 'Institut du Radium'. This three-storeyed yellow brick building, which stands in the district bounded by the venerable walls of the old Sorbonne and the tower of the new Jussieu University, was completed in 1914. Irène Curie, who was then nearly 17, helped her mother Marie to move the technical equipment, scientific journals, and test samples of radioactive material that had to be transported from the old laboratory in rue Cuvier to the new Radium Institute. World War One broke out a few days later.

The old, dark brown furniture is still *in situ*, and the antiquated-looking technical appliances have not been touched. Hélène Langevin pays only occasional visits to the old Radium Institute where her grandmother Marie Curie and her mother Irène carried out chemico-physical experiments. Herself a physicist, Irène Joliot-Curie's daughter works at a modern institute in Orsay. Speaking in the original laboratory, which has since been converted into a miniature museum, she recalls: 'My mother Irène was never in any doubt about her scientific vocation.'

At the beginning of the 20th century, when other girls and women still had to fight hard – against prejudices and prohibitions, parental and masculine opposition – for access to the study of the sciences, Irène Joliot-Curie's path was a smooth one. The inheritance she had to take up was quite different from theirs.

Her parents, Marie and Pierre Curie, had in 1903 been awarded a Nobel Prize for physics for the discovery of natural radioactivity, and Marie, the world's first female Nobel laureate, had in 1911 received a second Nobel Prize, this time for chemistry, on the stage of Stockholm's Royal Academy of Music. Seated among the spectators was Irène, then 14. She could not have guessed that she would likewise be awarded a Nobel Prize for chemistry in the same place almost a quarter of a century later.

Marie Curie was a devoted mother who carefully recorded her children's progress in her diaries, but she was also a professionally committed and successful scientist, hard on herself and very demanding of others. The untimely death of Pierre Curie, who was knocked down and killed by a horse-drawn wagon in 1906, brought Irène closer to her mother. Since Marie often attended conferences abroad and went away on lecture tours, Irène wrote her many affectionate letters during their separations. These not only recounted her daily activities but soon contained references to physical formulae.

Did Irène identify too closely with her mother? Hélène Langevin denies this. 'She simply loved the laboratory and scientific work, even when it failed to produce any major discoveries. She never laboured under the notion that she had to compete with her parents. She was far less infected with the spirit of competition than her mother Marie, who had been compelled to prevail against men in quite different circumstances.'

In Irène's case, her mother's example did not engender a psychological block of the kind so often found in the children of celebrated parents. She was, however, overshadowed by her at first.

Lise Meitner, a fellow physicist, encountered Irène in England in 1928, when the latter was 31. 'I formed the impression when we met at Cambridge that she was not – to ring the changes on an expression of Thomas Mann's – exempt from the difficulties of "daughterism". She seemed afraid of being regarded more as her mother's daughter than as a scientist in her own right.'

Not long before her death, Irène Joliot-Curie wrote this of their relationship: 'I was very much under the influence of my mother, whom I loved and profoundly admired, and could not throughout my childhood conceive of her having any human failings. I was quite different from her, however, being more like my father. This may be one of the reasons why we got on so well, although we sometimes took an entirely different view of things.'

Shortly after Irène's birth on 12 September 1897, Marie Curie reimmersed herself in her scientific research and started work on her doctoral thesis. Only a year after that, Marie and Pierre Curie were able to announce the discovery of two new radioactive elements: polonium and radium, substances occurring in uranium. In 1900 the Curie family moved from their apartment in rue de la Glacière to a small house in boulevard Kellerman. The Curies always employed Polish domestics so that Irène and her sister Eve, who was seven years younger, could learn Marie's mother tongue in addition to French. Marie's father-in-law, Dr Eugène Curie,

Marie and Pierre Curie with Irène in 1904

looked after little Irène during the day and remained her closest confidant until his death in 1910. Increasingly important to her after her father's death in 1906, he kindled her enthusiasm for botany as well as for Victor Hugo. She later conceded that he was also instrumental in shaping her political sentiments, her

EARLY CHILDHOOD

anticlericalism and her markedly down-to-earth approach to life.

After her husband's fatal accident Marie Curie rented a house in Sceaux, just south of Paris, whither she moved with her daughters and father-in-law. The girls were forbidden to mention their father to their mother, who seldom if ever spoke of him herself. Eve Curie's biography of her mother presents a detailed account of the freethinking education she bestowed on her daughters. Neither of them was ever baptized. They had to devote an hour each morning to some form of manual or mental labour. Thereafter they were sent out into the fresh air, where they played games and went for long walks. Marie Curie brought up her daughters to be as independent as possible, and they travelled on their own from the age of 12. It was always taken for granted that they would one day earn their own living.

The girls grew up in their mother's circle of acquaintances and colleagues, which included the physicists and mathematicians Jean Perrin, Paul Langevin, and André Debierne. They attached no importance to social etiquette. Eve Curie states that 20 years had to pass before it was brought home to her that life in society makes definite demands of its own, and that bidding someone good day is *de rigueur*. Irène Curie, who was far more reserved than her sister Eve, had difficulty in observing the social conventions throughout her life.

When Irène reached secondary school age, her mother founded a small private educational cooperative. Marie Curie considered the schooling of the day inadequate and needlessly overtaxing in its demands on children's time. She wanted what little Irène learned to be of practical value. Her educational experiment lasted two years, during which time Irène was privileged to count the greatest contemporary scientists among her teachers. In the mornings the small, mobile class of colleagues' children moved into the Sorbonne's laboratory, where Jean Perrin explained chemical processes to them. The next day they would travel to Fontenay-aux-Roses, where Paul Langevin taught them mathematics, and every Thursday afternoon they acquired new insights into the principles of physics from Marie Curie. But the curriculum also embraced literature, languages, and drawing taught by the academics and artists belonging to this circle of friends.

The hard-pressed parents abandoned their educational project after two years, not least because their pupils had to prepare for the official school examinations. Irène Curie went to the Collège Sevigné, the private school where she was to gain her baccalaureate. Eve Curie states in retrospect that the minor educational experiment did more to promote her sister's bent for science than any normal school could have done.

Irène Curie was thus introduced to the natural sciences at an early age and, so to speak, as a matter of course. After gaining her baccalaureate she continued her study of physics and mathematics at the Sorbonne, where her mother had held the chair of physics since her father's death. When she went to university, therefore, Irène attended her mother's lectures on physics, her own field of study.

Irène, who was staying in the country when World War One broke out, bombarded Marie with letters pestering her for permission to work beside her at the front. 'I hope I can make myself useful if I come to Paris,' she wrote to 'Mé', as she affectionately called her mother, on 1 October 1914. 'That is my dearest wish.'

Marie gave way, and she and Irène spent the next four years supervising the operation of twenty 'X-ray mobiles' or mobile X-ray units, as well as establishing some 200 stationary X-ray centres for the treatment of wounded soldiers. Irène learnt to use X-ray equipment, toured hospitals in various theatres of operations, and instructed nurses in radiography in Paris during the war years. This was probably when she first began to expose herself to excessive doses of radiation.

Irène worked long hours, because she was pursuing her study of physics and mathematics at the same time. When the war ended in 1918 she was appointed Marie's laboratory assistant at the Radium Institute. She was following in her mother's footsteps.

Although women had fought for and secured an improvement in their status in the educational system during the Third Republic (1870–1940) and had been admitted to universities in the 1880s, they were not admitted to professorships until after 1908, when Marie Curie became the first woman to obtain a chair at a French university.

Resistance to female competition from the conservative bastions of science remained strong, especially in the case of a distinguished woman scientist like Marie Curie. She stood for membership of the French Academy of Sciences but lost to the rival candidate, Edouard Branly, by the narrow second-ballot margin of 28 votes to 30. Although she was showered with other honours worldwide, Marie never stood for the Academy again.

But her daughter Irène construed this 'inheritance', too, as a challenge. In later years she ostentatiously stood for vacant places in the venerable Academy on two occasions – each time without success.

'To Irène Curie,' says her daughter Hélène Langevin, 'equality between man and woman was entirely natural.' She reacted very sharply if other people questioned that equality of status. Whenever it seemed appropriate to her and lay within her power, she spoke out and took the initiative on behalf of women's rights. Although it was easier for her to realize such aims than for other women of her day, she did her best to fulfil them for all.

Irène Curie was firmly resolved to embark on a scientific career as a physicist on becoming an assistant to her mother at the Radium Institute at the end of World War One. This cemented the already

Frédéric Joliot-Curie working on a Wilson cloud chamber in the laboratory of the Radium Institute, c.1930

close relationship between mother and daughter. Eve Curie reports that conversation at the lunch table was often limited to purely scientific discussions. Irène was a rather aloof character, unforth-coming toward strangers but very attached to her friends. She was uninterested in clothes and feminine fripperies, so those around her were doubly surprised when a love affair blossomed between her and Frédéric Joliot, who was three years her junior.

Born in Paris in 1900, Frédéric Joliot came from an upper-middle-class family and had studied physics and chemistry at a technical college. However, the newly fledged engineer showed more enthusiasm for scientific research than for its practical application. Not having attended an elite *École normale supérieure*, which in France was indispensable to a scientific career, he would have stood little chance of employment in a laboratory but for his former teacher, Paul Langevin. Langevin recommended him to

Marie Curie, who took him on as an assistant in 1923. Irène and Frédéric married three years later and subsequently adopted the double-barrelled name Joliot-Curie.

Their relationship, which took some time to mature, was not as surprising as all that. Irène opted for the same type of marriage as her mother, and was thus absolved from having to choose between work and love. The Joliot-Curies were united by love of their work and, in their private lives, by enjoyment of the countryside and athletic pursuits. They both detested urban life.

Frédéric Joliot is universally described as a brilliant and dynamic character, a scintillating conversationalist and man of charm with an invariable knack of winning people over to his side in argument – quite unlike his quiet and rather awkward wife. Irène's daughter, Hélène Langevin, confirms this difference between them: 'My parents were very complementary characters. Their collaboration was particularly effective for that reason.'

They were different but equal. In the scientific domain, their work together blended Irène's skill as a chemist and polonium expert with Frédéric the engineer's proficiency in physics. Marie Curie doubtless encouraged the relationship between the two young scientists in the hope of continuing and re-creating her own relationship with Pierre Curie.

Irène and Frédéric Joliot-Curie were burdened with the knowledge that they belonged to the elect. But Irène, having been accustomed to this idea from her childhood, displayed no signs of nervous strain and passed all her university examinations with ease. Her sister Eve recalls her at that period: 'This shy young person, deliberate and reserved of manner, had none of the outward effulgence peculiar to brilliant students. Her knowledge was permanently embedded in her well-ordered brain. To Irène, examination days on which even my mother had felt feverish and nervous were days like any other. She went calmly off to the Sorbonne, came back confident of having passed, and waited without any great emotion for a result that was guaranteed in advance.'

Irène Joliot-Curie obtained her doctorate in 1925. Her husband Frédéric, who belatedly graduated in 1927, obtained his in 1930. Their joint research in the field of radioactivity intensified from then onwards, a process unaffected by the birth of their daughter Hélène in 1927 and their son Pierre five years later.

The world of atomic physics had made immense strides in the previous 30 years. With the discovery of radioactivity, the idea of an atom as an unchanging indivisible particle was abandoned and a whole conception of the world was shattered. Years later, Irène Joliot-Curie summarized the importance of this discovery as follows:

'For the first time, one observed the spontaneous decay of an atom and its transmutation into the form of radiation accompanied by the release of energy. An atom of radium or polonium decays by simultaneously causing another atom to come into being; this transmutation is accompanied by an emission of heat. But the heat generated by one gram of radium is quite weak: in order to bring one litre of water to the boil in an hour, 700 grams of radium would be needed. Since one gram of radium cost approximately one million francs before the war, this process was not a particularly economical method of heating. Looked at from another angle, however, this exiguous generation of heat is remarkable. If coal is burnt, it undoubtedly heats far better than radium but is quickly consumed. Radium decays likewise – it is, in fact, the transmutation of its atoms that releases the heat – but it decays very slowly. It will take approximately 2,000 years for nearly all the atoms in a container to decay and transmute themselves into ordinary atoms of lead. In the course of its several thousand years of slow decay, one gram of radium develops as much heat as the burning of 400 kilograms of coal.'

Irène Joliot-Curie's account of the history of radioactivity goes on: 'During the early years of this century, some 40 radioactive elements were discovered in the natural world, and our knowledge of radiation and the structure of atoms made remarkable strides. It was ascertained that atoms consist of a tiny nucleus carrying a positive electrical charge and surrounded by negatively charged electrons. This nucleus is so small compared to the atom that, if we liken it to a small pea, the surrounding electrons would fill the Place de la Concorde.'

The nuclear physicists' passion for exploration was infectious, and they competed with one another in their research. Irène Joliot-Curie had begun her own research in the 1920s, at first alone, without her husband, and under her mother's supervision. The essential thing was to learn her trade, proceed methodically, and be thorough. She investigated the atomic weight of chlorine in several minerals and devoted her doctoral thesis to 'Research into the alpha rays of polonium', the radioactive material discovered by her parents.

In 1930 the German scientists Walther Bothe and Hans Becker observed a remarkable phenomenon. When they bombarded light elements like boron and beryllium with alpha rays, the irradiated substances emitted an extremely intense radiation that would even penetrate a sheet of lead ten centimetres thick. Although various explanations were advanced for the intensity of this radiation, none of them satisfied the Joliot-Curies. They jointly resolved to fathom the mystery.

The Joliot-Curies extracted the polonium required to produce the alpha radiation from the one-and-a-half grams of radium that Marie Curie jealously guarded at the Radium Institute. Having repeated the Bothe-Becker experiment, they discovered that the same amount of radiation as Bothe and Becker had used was capable of expelling protons (one of the particles in the nucleus of an atom) from paraffin while simultaneously projecting electrons into space with great force. They published these results, accompanied by scientific hypotheses, on 18 January 1932.

Their initial conjectures proved to be inadequate, but Irène and Frédéric Joliot-Curie did not give up. They continued to experiment with alpha rays, using them to bombard aluminium, fluorine, and natrium. Interim result: they succeeded in demonstrating that, contrary to previous assumptions, neutrons are somewhat lighter than protons. The next, crucial step: having further bombarded aluminium with alpha particles, they ascertained that the aluminium nuclei generated positrons (another subatomic particle, the antiparticle of the electron), which, although they remained in existence for a very short time, continued to emit radiation.

Irène Joliot-Curie's account of this discovery: 'If one exposes aluminium to alpha radiation, a radioactive element of approximately three minutes' duration is formed by transmutation.' Artificial radioactivity had been discovered. Until then, scientists had believed that all chemical elements born of atomic transmutations were stable, not radioactive. Irène and Frédéric Joliot-Curie's experiments had shown for the first time that radioactive elements could be created by artificial means.

On 15 January 1934, after conducting further experiments with boron and magnesium, all of which enabled them to extract new artificial substances, Irène and Frédéric Joliot-Curie reported their findings to the Academy of Sciences. In the following year, although strictly speaking physicists, they were awarded the Nobel Prize for chemistry because of their discovery's immense importance to that branch of science.

Irène, whose family had already brought home two Nobel Prizes, regarded the honour as recognition of her personal endeavours. At the age of 38, she had emerged from her mother's shadow. But her life did not change a great deal and she was unlikely to be over-whelmed by the honour. Having as a girl made the acquaintance of Albert Einstein, she probably fitted the picture she herself gave of Marie Curie in a newspaper article: 'The fact that my mother was not fond of socializing and did not seek to consort with influential people is often regarded as evidence of modesty. I tend to believe the opposite. She had a very precise idea of her own merits and did not consider it an honour to meet titled people or government ministers. I think she was very glad to have had the opportunity to meet Rudyard Kipling, but being presented to the Queen of Romania was a matter of complete indifference to her.'

The Joliot-Curies' great scientific success coincided with the death of Marie Curie in a sanatorium on 4 July 1934, at the age of 67. She died of leukaemia, undoubtedly as a consequence of a lifetime devoted to radioactive substances. Marie Curie stubbornly denied their dangers, so convinced was she of the exclusively beneficial use of radium in the treatment of cancer and radiotherapy. Although her daughter Irène continually warned against the political misuse of atomic research, she too played down the risks of the radiation to which scientists were personally exposed. 'Of my parents, it was certainly my father who realized the dangers of radioactivity earlier,' their daughter Hélène Langevin says today. She adds that Irène was hidebound by her upbringing in this respect.

In 1934/35 the family used part of the Nobel Prize money to build a new house at Sceaux, where their circle of friends and colleagues used to meet on Sundays. They now lived very much further from the Radium Institute than before. How did Irène Joliot-Curie cope with the twin burdens of work and family?

'The nature of scientific research was quite different then than it is now,' recalls her daughter Hélène, who married the grandson of Paul Langevin. 'Less time was spent in the laboratory, except at critical junctures. These days young female colleagues have to go to the crèche at six o'clock to collect their children; Irène never had to do that. I don't think she had any difficulty in reconciling her work with her family.' In addition, the university year allowed for long vacations which the family always spent in the mountains or at their house in Brittany. 'Besides,' says Hélène Langevin, 'my mother fell ill early on. She required treatment for tuberculosis soon after my birth, which meant that she had to rest a good deal. When she was at home, she was there for us and open to any suggestions.'

It never occurred to Irène Joliot-Curie, any more than it had to her mother Marie, to choose between her profession and her family, hence her unqualified support for other women's endeavours to earn a living and become financially independent. In 1937 she spoke in favour of this publicly: 'None of feminism's achievements is more important than the right of women to perform work for which they are qualified by their knowledge and aptitudes . . . Like men, not all women are the same; those who wish to undertake traditional tasks such as cooking, housekeeping and the rearing of children possess undeniable social utility, and whole professions are able to enlist their services. But the way must remain open for those who feel drawn to other activities.'

At that time the social and economic status of women in France was far from poor compared to that prevailing in other countries. But Frenchwomen lacked the basic political right to vote. 'For women to be truly on a par with men,' declared Irène Joliot-Curie, 'it is necessary and essential for them to participate in the country's political life. Women's suffrage is a question of principle, and questions of principle are most important.'

In 1936 Irène Joliot-Curie accepted an invitation to join Léon Blum's left-wing Popular Front government as undersecretary of state for scientific research. She, Cécile Brunschwig and Suzanne Lacore were the first women to become members of a French administration. She remained in office for only a few months – by prior agreement – so as at least to set an example. Irène never shrank from taking sides and making her opinions known. Her friend Angèle Pompéï attests that she had 'a passion for candour and clarity'.

In the mid 1930s the Joliot-Curies joined the Socialist Party. Sixty-two-year-old Hélène Langevin, a slim, energetic woman with short grey hair, has the following to say about her mother's political commitment: 'Irène shared my father's universal ideal of social justice and peace. She was a stickler in certain respects, but she also cherished a certain distrust of politics. Rather like her father Pierre, she felt that scientists weren't really qualified for them. She had an absolute horror of wasting her time at meetings and listening to interminable speeches that led to nothing. She always asked herself: Is what I'm doing effective?'

From 1937 onwards, when Irène was appointed a professor at the Sorbonne and Frédéric obtained a chair at the Collège de France, the couple worked separately with colleagues of their own.

In 1939, after the National Socialists had come to power in Germany, the Joliot-Curies abruptly ceased to publish their notable scientific findings. World War Two was looming, and sensational discoveries were being made in the field of physics: nuclear fission, which would later lead to the construction of the first atomic bomb.

Irène and Frédéric Joliot-Curie participated zealously in the research. Scientists had yet to be divided into hostile camps. In discovering artificial radioactivity, Irène and Frédéric Joliot-Curie had suggested bombarding atoms with neutrons instead of alpha rays. In 1938 Irène collaborated with her Yugoslav colleague Pavlo Savitch in applying this technique to the uranium atom. Instead of the transuranian element they had been expecting (an element with an atomic number higher than uranium), they succeeded in identifying an element similar to lanthanum. In Sweden this discovery led Lise Meitner and Otto Frisch to surmise that atomic nuclei of the bombarded uranium, instead of being transmuted into transuranian nuclei, disintegrated into fragments. This furnished Otto Hahn and Fritz Strassmann, who had demonstrated nuclear fission by purely chemical means in Berlin in December 1938, with a physical explanation. There was no further doubt that nuclear fission had been accomplished.

Irène Joliot-Curie outlined the significance of this achievement, to which she herself had contributed, as follows: 'Monsieur Joliot and I discovered in 1934 that radioactive elements can be manufactured by transmutation. Research into artificial radioactivity has progressed so extraordinarily fast that we are now acquainted with several hundred new elements of this kind. But a serviceable amount of atomic energy could not be released by the methods employed hitherto. The energy released by artificial transmutation or by the radioelements formed was considerably less than the energy required by the equipment needed for transmutation. It was the phenomenon of "fission", which was discovered by Hahn and Strassmann . . . , that was to change this situation.'

In 1939 Frédéric Joliot-Curie began nuclear fission experiments in his laboratory and tried to measure the energy released by splitting the atomic nucleus of uranium: approximately 200 million electron volts, which became transmuted into thermal energy. He now conjectured that bombarding an atomic nucleus with neutrons, which thereupon disintegrated into two fragments, led to the emission of further neutrons, which would in turn bombard other nuclei. He showed that these explosions were released in series and that you could artificially control such chain reactions by slowing the neutrons down. He and his colleagues Hans Halban and Lew Kowalski had identified the principles whereby energy and atomic explosive force could be obtained from atomic power. It was precisely then that World War Two broke out in Europe.

Frédéric Joliot-Curie joined the Resistance during the German occupation of France. Although Irène shared his political stance and approved of his activities, she did not choose to tread the same path. Unlike her husband, who was propelled into the limelight by political circumstances, she was less active during the war years.

Irène Joliot-Curie had been displaying incipient signs of illness caused by radiation since the end of the 1930s. According to her daughter Hélène Langevin, however, it was not consideration for her health or her family that prompted her to take things easier. She was averse to becoming politically organized and involved again in party politics. She felt that her only meaningful commitment lay in the scientific domain and her aspirations there were denied during the war years. The Radium Institute was merely ticking over, and our biographical information about Irène Joliot-Curie during those dark days is sparse.

In September 1939 Frédéric Joliot-Curie was called up and assigned the rank of captain of artillery, the intention being that he should continue his scientific research under military aegis at a makeshift laboratory in Clermont-Ferrand. The family moved there with him. His main concern was the uranium that had been accumulated for experimental purposes and the 26 containers of heavy water specially acquired from Norway for the retarding of neutrons. If that material had fallen into German hands it might have given them a lead in atomic bomb research. The chemical water was dispatched to England with Joliot's associates, Halban and Kowalski, the uranium cached near Toulouse.

The Germans had already broken into the chemical laboratory at the Collège de France by the time the Joliot-Curie family returned to Paris in September 1940. Frédéric was questioned about the location of the containers and the uranium, but he adroitly denied all knowledge of it. The occupying power earmarked his chemical laboratory at the Collège de France for research purposes and assigned four young German physicists to work there under his direction.

In 1942 Frédéric joined the Communist Party. His laboratory had for some time been engaged in clandestine activities quite different from those it was permitted to undertake. Unbeknown to the Germans conducting research there, Frédéric's small Resistance cell was secretly producing Molotov cocktails and radio receivers. Early in 1944 the situation became critical, and for six weeks Frédéric's family had to remain in hiding at a country hotel while Frédéric himself went underground in Paris under an assumed name. Thereafter Irène and her two children fled to Switzerland to avoid German reprisals.

Hélène Langevin recalls that her mother refused to be parted, even when in hiding, from her logarithm tables with 'Radium Institute' inscribed in the margin. Irène Joliot-Curie had never spent any lengthy periods away from the Institute at any stage in her life.

Irène's exile with the children and her husband's clandestine existence did not last long. Paris was liberated in the same year. On 25 August 1944, some two months after the Allied landing in Normandy, the French capital's war came to an end. The eastern part of the country had yet to be liberated, but political life was already reconstituting itself under the leadership of General de Gaulle. Among other measures introduced in 1944, women were finally granted the vote. Politics had a leftward slant. Those who had collaborated with the Vichy regime, the French pseudo-government in power under the German occupation, were brought to trial. Anyone who had been in the Resistance suddenly acquired a host of friends. This applied to Irène and Frédéric Joliot-Curie. The couple had already belonged to their country's scientific elite before the war, but Frédéric's Resistance activities rendered them doubly welcome after their return from exile and the underground respectively.

The provisional government headed by General de Gaulle, the military strategist of the Resistance's non-communist minority, filled the key positions in the country's political administration. Frédéric Joliot-Curie was appointed director of the most important government research institute, the *Centre National de la Recherche Scientifique* (National Centre for Scientific Research), or CNRS. He persuaded de Gaulle to set up an atomic energy authority, the *Commissariat à l'Énergie Atomique* (Atomic Energy Commission), or CEA, whose high commissioner he became in 1945. He was assisted in this post by three commissioners, one of whom was Irène, so the couple were briefly able to combine their political and scientific commitments.

The CEA's task was to embark on the development of atomic energy. Much progress had been made abroad during the war years. On 2 December 1942 the Italian scientist Enrico Fermi had activated the first atomic pile at the University of Chicago. France made a belated start but was all the keener to catch up, and would eventually become Europe's first atomic power. That still lay in the future, however. It was not until 15 December 1948 that Frédéric Joliot-Curie brought the first French reactor (ZOE) into operation.

Atomic energy was still regarded with some scepticism at that time. 'A new era is opening up for mankind,' Irène Joliot-Curie declared when lecturing on 'Radioactivity and Atomic Energy' in 1948. She believed in the peaceful uses of this novel source of energy. 'That is why every effort must be made to explore this unknown field so as to use it for the benefit of humanity.' Like other scientists of the time, she was almost unaware of the dangers atomic energy posed to the civil population.

Irène's misgivings pointed in another direction. She doubtless realized that there were strings attached to the peaceful use of atomic energy. Two atomic bombs had been detonated, one above the Japanese city of Hiroshima on 6 August 1945 and another above Nagasaki three days later. 'It grieves us that a great country like the USA is squandering all its energies on augmenting the destructive power of atomic bombs,' she said in the same lecture, 'while neglecting other major problems of universal interest.' The events of World War Two had taught her to fear the misuse of scientific research. If another war broke out, she warned, it would be a nuclear war.

While Frédéric Joliot-Curie remained vehemently committed to the Communist Party and the peace movement, Irène joined the *Union des Femmes Françaises* (French Women's Union). Although politically independent, this women's association was close to the Communist Party.

Like other scientists and intellectuals of her day, Irène attended events and conferences sponsored by the international peace movement. In 1948, for example, she accompanied Pablo Picasso to an international congress at Wrocław in Poland, but she never, as her husband did, committed herself to such organizations by accepting posts or other functions in them. Irène Joliot-Curie preferred to express her sympathies by means of supportive appearances, lectures, and articles.

In 1948 she undertook a tour of the United States in aid of a press campaign by the American committee for the support of refugees of the Spanish Civil War. She had visited the USA once before with her mother, Marie Curie, in 1921. When she reached New York on 19 March 1948, the US authorities detained her on Ellis Island for a whole day before permitting her to resume her journey. To anti-communist America in the early days of the McCarthy era, she was politically suspect.

Writing to her husband 'Fred' on 26 March 1948, she described the circumstances surrounding her journey and poked fun at her own aversion to publicity: 'I'm less tired than I feared. The press conference method is a definite improvement on the system prevailing during my trip with Mé, when we were continually requested to grant interviews to journalists or photographers. Now they all turn up at once, and one doesn't have to repeat the same thing fifty times over. Press conferences are definitely becoming my element, and I'm wondering how I shall manage without them when I return to France.'

Irène Joliot-Curie was never wholly engrossed in political activities, as her husband was, and her duties as a commissioner of the CEA did not preoccupy her completely. She continued to spend a large part of her time in her laboratory at the Radium Institute, whose director she was finally appointed in 1946.

But the couple were soon isolated by their communist sympathies. The Cold War had begun, and France had joined NATO, the western defensive alliance whose official doctrine embraced anti-communism and a strategy based on nuclear deterrence. A communist high commissioner of the supreme French atomic energy authority, who had already publicized his opposition to the building of a French atomic bomb, was no longer wanted.

Frédéric Joliot-Curie was relieved of his post on 19 March 1950. The CEA, which he himself had founded as a believer in pacifism, became one of the most powerful institutions in the country – a country that would ultimately possess a large number of nuclear power stations and develop nuclear weapons of its own. Irène Joliot-Curie's term of office as an atomic commissioner expired in 1951 and was not renewed. The friends who used to visit the house in Sceaux on Sunday afternoons became fewer in number.

Irène devoted herself again to her teaching activities at the Sorbonne and the running of the Radium Institute, although her health was rapidly deteriorating. She had to undergo several operations, and her husband was suffering from liver disease.

In 1955 she inaugurated plans for a new institute of nuclear physics at Orsay, near Paris. The Radium Institute's technological equipment had long ceased to be adequate, and she dreamed – as Marie Curie had done before her – of more modern working

Frédéric and Irène Joliot-Curie at Courchevel in Savoy, 1955

conditions. Her daughter Hélène Langevin's present place of work at Orsay would have fulfilled her expectations.

Before long, even Irène's beloved walks became too much for her – 'I think I'm getting lazy,' she said in her laconic way – so her friend Angèle Pompéï took her for drives instead. Eventually admitted to hospital, she died of leukaemia on 17 March 1956, at the age of only 58. The French government grudgingly accorded her a state funeral. Frédéric Joliot-Curie died a year later. The names of the two scientists had been expunged from France's official scientific records for almost two decades.

Irène Joliot-Curie had defined her conception of a scientist's role in a school radio broadcast in 1938: 'I believe that what constitutes true scientific research is the disinterested thirst for knowledge it is meant to assuage; a paradoxical fact, because it is, after all, this type of work that ultimately has the most sensational practical results . . . Nearly all the inventions that have transformed the life of humanity in the past two centuries were preceded by a scientist's laboratory experiment which at first seemed wholly useless.'

Irène Joliot-Curie also described her research work as a vocation and a passion: 'One element of success, whatever one's profession, is pleasure in one's craft, but I believe that this applies particularly to scientific work. Science has something in common with art in this respect: knowledge and intelligence without love of research do not make a scholar, any more than naturally occurring talent plus study make an artist out of someone without a love of art.'

Notes

1 Eve Curie, *Madame Curie*, (London: 1938), p. 48.
2 Marie Curie, *Pierre Curie* (New York: 1923), p. 78.
3 Curie, *Pierre Curie*, p. 159.
4 Curie, *Madame Curie*, p. 36.
5 Curie, *Madame Curie*, p. 43.
6 Susan Quinn, *Marie Curie: A Life* (London: 1995), p. 63.
7 Quinn, *Marie Curie*, p. 63.
8 Curie, *Pierre Curie*, p. 68.
9 Curie, *Madame Curie*, pp. 82–3.
10 Curie, *Madame Curie*, p. 73.
11 Curie, *Pierre Curie*, p. 82.
12 Quinn, *Marie Curie*, p. 75.
13 Curie, *Pierre Curie*, pp. 82–3.
14 Curie, *Madame Curie*, pp. 86–7.
15 Curie, *Madame Curie*, pp. 87–8.
16 Curie, *Madame Curie*, p. 92.
17 Curie, *Madame Curie*, p. 110.
18 Curie, *Pierre Curie*, p. 85.
19 Curie, *Pierre Curie*, p. 84.
20 Curie, *Pierre Curie*, p. 85.
21 Curie, *Pierre Curie*, p. 85.
22 Curie, *Madame Curie*, p. 119.
23 Curie, *Pierre Curie*, p. 85.
24 Curie, *Pierre Curie*, p. 34.
25 Curie, *Pierre Curie*, p. 19.
26 Curie, *Madame Curie*, p. 136.
27 Curie, *Madame Curie*, p. 142.
28 Curie, *Madame Curie*, p. 142.
29 Curie, *Madame Curie*, p. 154.
30 Curie, *Madame Curie*, p. 153.
31 Curie, *Madame Curie*, p. 155.
32 Curie, *Madame Curie*, p. 156.
33 Curie, *Madame Curie*, p. 157.
34 Eve, *A S Rutherford* (New York: 1939), p. 37.
35 Quinn, *Marie Curie*, p. 406.
36 Curie, *Madame Curie*, p. 169.
37 Curie, *Madame Curie*, p. 171.
38 Curie, *Madame Curie*, p. 171.
39 Curie, *Madame Curie*, p. 171.
40 Curie, *Pierre Curie*, p. 45.
41 Alex Keller, *The Infancy of Atomic Physics* (Oxford: 1983), p. 75.
42 Curie, *Pierre Curie*, p. 47.
43 Curie, *Pierre Curie*, p. 91.
44 Robert Reid, *Marie Curie* (London: 1974), p. 95.
45 Curie, *Pierre Curie*, p. 92.
46 Curie, *Pierre Curie*, p. 91.
47 Henry Paul, *From Knowledge to Power* (Cambridge: 1985), p. 145.
48 Curie, *Pierre Curie*, p. 90.
49 Curie, *Pierre Curie*, p. 90.
50 Curie, *Madame Curie*, p. 179.
51 Curie, *Madame Curie*, p. 181.
52 Curie, *Madame Curie*, p. 181.
53 Cited in J L Davis, 'The Research School of Marie Curie in the Paris Faculty, 1907–1914', *Annals of Science*, 52, 1995, p. 322.
54 Curie, *Pierre Curie*, p. 48.
55 Curie, *Pierre Curie*, pp. 103–4.
56 Curie, *Madame Curie*, pp. 205–6.
57 See Soraya Boudia, 'The Curie Laboratory: Radioactivity and Metrology', *History and Technology*, Vol. 13, 1997, pp. 250–51; and Xavier Roqué, 'Marie Curie and the Radium Industry', pp. 270–71.
58 David Wilson, *Rutherford: Simple Genius* (Cambridge MA: 1983), p. 147.
59 Ernest Rutherford, *Radioactivity*, (Cambridge: 1905), p. 439.
60 Curie and Curie, 'Sur les corps radio-actifs', cited in Alfred Romer, *Radiochemistry and the Discovery of Isotopes* (New York: 1964), p. 122.
61 Curie and Curie, 'Sur les corps radio-actifs', cited in Romer, *Radiochemistry*, p. 122.
62 Marie Curie, 'Radium and Radioactivity' *Century Magazine* (January 1904), pp. 461–6.
63 Curie and Curie, 'Sur les corps radio-actifs', cited in Romer, *Radiochemistry*, p. 121.
64 Romer, *Radiochemistry*, p. 123.
65 Rutherford and Soddy, 'The Cause and Nature of Radioactivity', *Philosophical Magazine* 4, pp. 370–96 (1902).
66 Wilson, *Rutherford*, p. 158.
67 Rutherford and Soddy, 'The Cause

and Nature of Radioactivity',
Philosophical Magazine 4, (1902)
pp. 370–96.

68 Frederick Soddy, *Interpretation of Radium*, (London: 1909)
pp. 230–231.

69 Soddy, *Interpretation*, p. 250.

70 From the Curie archives at the Institut Curie.

71 Strutt, Hon R J, *The Becquerel Rays and the Properties of Radium* (London: 1904) p. 53.

72 Strutt, *Becquerel Rays*, pp. 189.

73 Curie, *Madame Curie*, p. 207–8.

74 Curie, *Madame Curie*, p. 214.

75 Curie, *Pierre Curie*, p. 92.

76 Curie, *Madame Curie*, p. 188.

77 Cited in Quinn, *Marie Curie*, p. 215.

78 Curie, *Madame Curie*, p. 196.

79 Curie, *Pierre Curie*, p. 169.

80 Cited in Quinn, *Marie Curie*, p. 183 from 'The Sole Meeting of Pierre Curie and Ernest Rutherford,' *The Lancet*, 21 November 1907.

81 Curie, *Madame Curie*, p. 199.

82 Cited in Quinn, *Marie Curie*, p. 189 from Mittag-Leffler Institute, Djursholm, Sweden.

83 Curie, *Madame Curie*, p. 221.

84 Curie, *Madame Curie*, p. 221.

85 1903 Nobel Physics Prize presentation speech.

86 Cited in Elizabeth Crawford, *The Beginnings of the Nobel Institution*, p. 195, from *La Semaine*, 20 December 1903.

87 Curie, *Madame Curie*, p. 227.

88 Curie, *Madame Curie*, pp. 248–9.

89 Curie, *Madame Curie*, pp. 247.

90 Curie, *Madame Curie*, p. 252.

91 Curie, *Madame Curie*, p. 226.

92 Curie, *Madame Curie*, p. 238.

93 Pierre Curie Nobel Lecture, 6 June 1905.

94 Cited in Quinn, *Marie Curie*, p. 226, from Pierre Curie to George Gouy, 14 April 1905.

95 From Marie Curie's mourning journal, cited in Quinn, *Marie Curie*, p. 231.

96 Curie, *Madame Curie*, p. 256.

97 From mourning journal, cited in Quinn, *Marie Curie*, p. 237.

98 Curie, *Madame Curie*, p. 261.

99 From mourning journal, cited in Quinn, *Marie Curie*, p. 240.

100 From mourning journal, cited in Quinn, *Marie Curie*, p. 239.

101 Curie, *Madame Curie*, p. 267.

102 Curie, *Madame Curie*, p. 272.

103 Curie, *Madame Curie*, p. 276.

104 Curie, *Madame Curie*, p. 276.

105 Albert Einstein 'Paul Langevin', *La Pensée*, 12, May June 1947, pp. 13–14.

106 Camille Marbo, *À travers deux siècles 1883–1967* (Paris: 1968), p. 107.

104 Undated item in the archives of the EPCI, cited in Quinn, *Marie Curie*, p. 260.

108 Marie Curie to Ellen Gleditsch, 17 August 1908, Royal University Library, Oslo, Norway, cited in Quinn, *Marie Curie*, p. 253.

109 Irène Curie to Marie Curie, Arromanches 1907, *Marie-Irène Curie Correspondence*, ed. Ziegler (Paris: 1974), p. 19.

110 Cited in Quinn, *Marie Curie*, p. 255.

111 Cited in Boudia, 'Radioactivity and Metrology', p. 257.

112 Rosalynd Pflaum, *Grand Obsession: Marie Curie and her World* (New York: 1989), p. 156.

113 Rutherford to Boltwood, 21 October 1911, in Lawrence Badash, ed. *Rutherford and Boltwood: Letters on Radioactivity* (New Haven: 1969).

114 Cited in Reid, *Marie Curie*, p. 197.

115 'A New Affair' *L'Intransigeant*, 19 November 1911, cited in Quinn, *Marie Curie*, p. 315.

116 *L'Intransigeant*, 20 November 1911, cited in Quinn, *Marie Curie*, p. 316.

117 *Le Temps*, 8 November 1911, cited in Quinn, *Marie Curie*, p. 307.

118 From 'Correspondence concerning the Nobel prize in chemistry of Marie Curie, 1911', in the manuscript collection of the Royal Academy of Sciences, Centre for History of Science, Stockholm, Sweden, cited in Quinn, *Marie Curie*, p. 309.

119 Jacques Curie to Marie Curie, 6 November 1911, archives of the EPCI, cited in Quinn, *Marie Curie*, p. 311.

120 Cited in Quinn, *Marie Curie*, p. 310.

121 Albert Einstein to Marie Curie, 23 November 1911, Countway Library,

Harvard University, as cited in
Quinn, *Marie Curie*, p. 310.

122 Loie Fuller to Marie Curie, 17
November 1911, archives of the EPCI,
as cited in Quinn, *Marie Curie*, p. 310.

123 *L'Oeuvre*, 23 November 1911, as cited
in Quinn, *Marie Curie*, p. 269.

124 Jacques Curie to Marie Curie, 27
December 1911, archives of the EPCI,
cited in Quinn, *Marie Curie*, p. 317.

125 *L'Action française*, 22 November 1911,
cited in Quinn, *Marie Curie*, p. 318.

126 Marbo, *À travers*, p. 109.

127 Svante Arrhenius to Marie Curie,
1 December 1911, Mittag-Leffler
Institute, Djursholm, cited in Quinn,
Marie Curie, p. 327.

128 Marie Curie to Svante Arrhenius,
5 December 1911, Royal Academy of
Sciences, Centre for the History of
Science, Stockholm Sweden, cited in
Quinn, *Marie Curie*, p. 328.

129 Marie Curie 1911 Nobel acceptance
speech.

130 Sir William Thomson, *Popular
Lectures and Addresses* (London and
New York: 1891–4).

131 Marie Curie 1911 Nobel acceptance
speech.

132 Marie Curie to Irène Curie, 6 August
1911, cited in Curie, *Madame Curie*,
p. 302.

133 Irène Curie to Marie Curie, 3 August
1911, cited in Reid, *Marie Curie*, p. 229.

134 Marie Curie to Irène Curie, 6 August
1911, cited in Curie, *Madame Curie*,
p. 304.

135 Cited in Quinn, *Marie Curie*, p. 379.

136 Curie, *Pierre Curie*, pp. 103–4.

137 Curie, *La Radiologie et la Guerre*
(Paris: 1921) pp. 37–40.

138 Irène Curie to Marie Curie,
16 September 1915, in Marie Curie,
Marie–Irène Correspondence, ed. Ziegler
(Paris: 1974).

139 Marie Curie to Paul Langevin,
1 January 1915, cited in Curie,
Madame Curie, p. 310.

140 Reid, *Marie Curie*, p. 239.

141 Irène Curie to Marie Curie, 3 August
1917, cited in Curie, *Marie–Irène
Correspondence*.

142 Curie, *Pierre Curie*, p. 106.

143 Curie, *La Radiologie et la Guerre*,

pp. 37–40.

144 Curie, *La Radiologie et la Guerre*,
pp. 37–40.

145 Lawrence Badash, *Radioactivity in
America* (Baltimore: 1979) p. 149.

146 Marie Meloney to Marie Curie, 16
September 1920, cited in Reid, *Marie
Curie*, p. 252.

147 Pierre Roché to Marie Meloney, 8
January 1921, Columbia University
Library, cited in Reid, *Marie Curie*,
p. 252.

148 Marie Meloney to Marie Curie, 23
March 1921, cited in Reid, *Marie Curie*,
p. 254.

149 Quinn, *Marie Curie*, p. 391.

150 *The Delineator*, June 1921, cited in
Quinn, *Marie Curie*, p. 388.

151 *New York City Evening World*, 12 May
1921, cited in Reid, *Marie Curie*, p. 262.

152 Curie, *Madame Curie*, p. 346.

153 Bertram Boltwood to Ernest
Rutherford, 5 December 1911, in
Badash, ed. *Rutherford and Boltwood*.

154 Bertram Boltwood to Ernest
Rutherford, 16 July 1921, in Badash,
ed. *Rutherford and Boltwood*.

155 Curie, *Madame Curie*, p. 355.

156 Marie Curie to Józef Skłodowski,
December 1920, cited in Curie,
Madame Curie, p. 318.

157 Curie, *Madame Curie*, p. 386.

158 *La Liberté*, 12 December 1903, cited in
Quinn, *Marie Curie*, p. 416.

159 Irène Curie to Marie Curie, 5 August
1907, cited in Quinn, *Marie Curie*,
p. 415.

160 Marie Curie to Harlan S Miner, 29
May 1925, cited in Quinn, *Marie Curie*,
p. 413.

161 Curie, *Madame Curie*, p. 368.

162 Cited in Quinn, *Marie Curie*, p. 256.

163 Curie, *Madame Curie*, pp. 373–4.

164 *Le Quotidien*, 31 March 1925, cited in
Pflaum, *Grand Obsession*, p. 259.

165 Curie, *Madame Curie*, p. 327.

166 Curie, *Madame Curie*, p. 329.

167 Marlene and Geoffrey Rayner-
Canham, *Devotion* (Quebec: 1997),
p. 77.

168 Cited in Quinn, *Marie Curie*, p. 404.

169 Curie, *Madame Curie*, p. 372.

170 Curie, *Madame Curie*, p. 373.

Chronology

Year	History	Culture
1867	Prussia forms North German Confederation. Austria forms Austro-Hungarian empire. US purchases Alaska from Russia. Meiji Restoration in Japan; end of shogunates. Joseph Lister introduces antiseptic surgery.	Giuseppe Verdi, *Don Carlos*. Joseph Strauss, *The Blue Danube*. Karl Marx, *Das Kapital*. Henrik Ibsen, *Peer Gynt*.
1876	China declares Korea an independent state. Turkish massacre of Bulgarians. Battle of Little Bighorn; General Custer dies. Alexander Graham Bell invents telephone.	Johannes Brahms, *First Symphony*. Richard Wagner, *Siegfried*. First complete performance of Wagner's *The Ring*.
1877	Queen Victoria proclaimed empress of India. Russo-Turkish war. Britain annexes Transvaal. Porfirio Diaz becomes president of Mexico. In Japan, Satsuma rebellion suppressed.	Émile Zola, *L'Assommoir*.
1878	Congress of Berlin resolves Balkan crisis. In Britain, Salvation Army created. Serbia becomes independent. Britain gains Cyprus. Britain fights second Afghan War (until 1880). Electric street lighting in London.	Pyotr Ilyich Tchaikovsky, *Swan Lake*.
1880	In Britain, William Gladstone becomes prime minister. First Boer War (until 1881). Pasteur discovers streptococcus.	Tchaikovsky, *1812 Overture*. Fyodor Dostoevsky, *The Brothers Karamazov*.
1883	Jewish immigration to Palestine (Rothschild Colonies). Germany acquires SW Africa. In Chicago, world's first skyscraper built.	Robert Louis Stevenson, *Treasure Island*. Friedrich Nietzsche, *Thus Spake Zarathustra*.
1886	In Cuba, slavery abolished. Tunisia becomes French protectorate. First meeting of Indian National Congress.	Stevenson, *Dr Jekyll and Mr Hyde*. Arthur Rimbaud, *Les Illuminations*.
1889	Second Socialist International. Italy invades Somalia and Ethiopia. In Paris, Eiffel Tower completed. Brazil proclaims itself a republic.	Verdi, *Falstaff*. George Bernard Shaw, *Fabian Essays*.
1891	Building of Trans-Siberian railway begins. Shearers' strike in Australia.	Oscar Wilde, *The Picture of Dorian Gray*.

Year	Age	Life
1893	26	Marie graduates first in her class at the Sorbonne with a *licence* (roughly equivalent to a master's degree) in physical sciences. Receives Alexandrovitch scholarship for an additional year of study in mathematics.
1894	27	Marie meets Pierre. She graduates second for the licence in mathematics.
1895	28	Marie and Pierre are married in a simple ceremony at Sceaux. Marie's father and siblings attend. Pierre is appointed professor at the EPCI.
1896	29	Marie awarded agrégation.
1897	30	Irène Curie is born. Marie chooses to make uranium rays the subject of her doctoral dissertation. Begins testing samples in a disused machine shop at the EPCI. Curie publishes her first paper, 'Magnetic Properties of Tempered Steel'.
1898	31	February: Marie tests pitchblende using a piezoelectric quartz electrometer. Marie and Pierre publish 'On a new, radioactive substance contained in pitchblende', on the discovery of polonium. It is the first time the word 'radioactive' is used. Marie is awarded the *prix Gegner* (she will be awarded it twice more, in 1900 and 1902). December: Marie Curie, Pierre Curie, and Gustave Bémont publish on the discovery of radium, in 'On a new, strongly radioactive substance contained in pitchblende'. First explicit mention of radioactivity as an atomic property.
1899	32	Ten tonnes of pitchblende from St Joachimsthal mine arrive at the EPCI. In conjunction with the services of the *Société Centrale des Produits Chimiques*, Marie and Pierre begin purifying it in a hangar, previously a dissecting room for the School of Medicine. André Debierne, a collaborator of the Curies, discovers actinium.

Year	History	Culture
1893	Franco-Russian alliance signed. South Africa Company launches Matabele War. France annexes Laos.	Antonín Dvorák, *From the New World*. Tchaikovsky, *Pathétique*. Wilde, *A Woman of No Importance*.
1894	French President Carnot assassinated. In France, Alfred Dreyfus convicted of treason. In Russia, Nicholas II becomes tsar (until 1917). Sino-Japanese war (until 1895). In US, Pullman strike.	Claude Debussy, *L'Après-midi d'un faune*. Rudyard Kipling, *The Jungle Book*. G B Shaw, *Arms and the Man*.
1895	In Britain, Lord Salisbury becomes prime minister. Cuban rebellion begins. Japan conquers Taiwan (Formosa). Guglielmo Marconi invents wireless telegraphy. Wilhelm Röntgen discovers X-rays.	H G Wells, *The Time Machine*. W B Yeats, *Poems*. Wilde, *The Importance of Being Earnest*.
1896	Theodore Herzl founds Zionism. First Olympic Games of the modern era held in Athens. Antoine (Henri) Becquerel discovers radioactivity.	Giacomo Puccini, *La Bohème*. Thomas Hardy, *Jude the Obscure*.
1897	Queen Victoria celebrates Diamond Jubilee. In France, Dreyfus affair. Britain destroys Benin City. Klondike gold rush (until 1899). Lord Kelvin shows that uranium rays 'electrify' the air. J J Thomson discovers the electron.	Joseph Conrad, *The Nigger of the Narcissus*. Stefan George, *Das Jahr der Seele*. August Strindberg, *Inferno*. Edmond Rostand, *Cyrano de Bergerac*.
1898	Spanish-American war: Spain loses Cuba, Puerto Rico, and the Philippines. Britain conquers Sudan.	Henry James, *The Turn of the Screw*. H G Wells, *The War of the Worlds*. Zola, *J'Accuse*. Auguste Rodin, *The Kiss*.
1899	Second Boer War (until 1902). Dreyfus pardoned. Relief of Mafeking. In China, Boxer Rebellion (until 1901). Aspirin introduced. Ernest Rutherford publishes a paper describing what he names the alpha and beta rays emitted from radioactive substances.	Hector Berlioz, *The Taking of Troy*. Edward Elgar, *Enigma Variations*. George, *Der Teppich des Lebens*.

Year	Age	Life
1900	33	Pierre turns down a position at the University of Geneva. Poincaré gets Pierre appointed to teach a course in physics at the Sorbonne. Marie becomes first female teacher at the *École normale supérieure* at Sèvres, the best women's teacher training school in France.
1901	34	Pierre is awarded the *prix La Caze*, worth 10,000 francs.
1902	35	May: Marie's father dies in Warsaw. July: Marie announces the isolation of a decigram of radium, enough to determine its atomic weight at 225 (the current accepted value is 226).
1903	36	June: Marie defends her dissertation at the Sorbonne. August: Marie suffers a miscarriage in her fifth month of pregnancy. November: Marie and Pierre receive the Humphrey Davy medal from the Royal Society of London. Marie and Pierre learn that they have one half of the Nobel Prize for physics. The other half goes to Henri Becquerel.
1904	37	First issue of *Le Radium* published. Pierre is appointed professor at the Sorbonne. Marie becomes his assistant. It is the first time she receives a salary for her scientific work. Eve, a second daughter, is born.
1905	38	Pierre is elected to the French Academy of Sciences. He delivers the Nobel lecture in Stockholm.
1906	39	April: Pierre is killed by a horse-drawn carriage on rue Dauphine. Marie takes over his chair at the Sorbonne.
1907	40	Marie starts cooperative school for Irène and other children.
1910	43	Pierre's father Eugene dies. The International Congress of Radiology and Electricity in Brussels resolves to adopt Marie Curie's unit, the curie, for the international radiation standard.
1911	44	Marie fails to gain election to the Academy of Sciences. Attends the first Solvay Congress. Her affair with Paul Langevin is revealed in the press. She wins a second Nobel Prize for chemistry, travels to Stockholm to deliver acceptance speech. She collapses on her return to Paris due to kidney infection.
1914	47	Radium Institute in Paris is completed.

Year	History	Culture
1900	First Pan-African Conference. First Zeppelin flight. Universal Exposition takes place in Paris; 50 million visitors attend.	Puccini, *Tosca*. Conrad, *Lord Jim*. Sigmund Freud, *The Interpretation of Dreams*.
1901	Queen Victoria dies; Edward VII becomes king. US President William McKinley assassinated; Theodore Roosevelt becomes president.	Strindberg, *The Dance of Death*. Kipling, *Kim*. Anton Chekhov, *The Three Sisters*. Pablo Picasso begins Blue Period (until 1904).
1902	Peace of Vereeniging ends Boer War. Anglo-Japanese alliance. Rutherford and Soddy publish 'The Cause and Nature of Radioactivity', in which they state that 'radioactivity is a manifestation of sub-atomic chemical change.'	Debussy, *Pelléas et Mélisande*. Hillaire Belloc, *The Path to Rome*. Arthur Conan Doyle, *The Hound of the Baskervilles*. Conrad, *The Heart of Darkness*. Claude Monet, *Waterloo Bridge*.
1903	Bolshevik-Menshevik split in Communist Party of Russia. Pogroms against Jews in Russia. Suffragette movement begins in Britain. Panama Canal Zone granted to US to build and manage waterway. Wright Brothers' first flight.	Henry James, *The Ambassadors*.
1904	France and Britain sign Entente Cordiale. Russo-Japanese War. Photoelectric cell invented.	Puccini, *Madama Butterfly*. J M Barrie, *Peter Pan*. Chekhov, *The Cherry Orchard*.
1905	Russian revolution against monarchy fails. Bloody Sunday massacre. Korea becomes protectorate of Japan.	Albert Einstein, *Special Theory of Relativity*. Paul Cézanne, *Les Grandes baigneuses*.
1906	Algeciras Conference resolves dispute between France and Germany over Morocco. Duma created in Russia. Revolution in Iran.	Henri Matisse, *Bonheur de vivre*. Maxim Gorky, *The Mother* (until 1907).
1907	Anglo-Russian Entente. Electric washing-machine invented.	Conrad, *The Secret Agent*. Rainer Maria Rilke, *Neue Gedichte*.
1910	In Britain, George V becomes king. Union of South Africa created. Japan annexes Korea.	Igor Stravinsky, *The Firebird*. Post-impressionist exhibition, London.
1911	Parliament Act resolves constitutional crisis in Britain. Chinese revolution against imperial dynasties. Ernest Rutherford puts forward the nuclear model of the atom.	Richard Strauss, *Der Rosenkavalier*.
1914	28 June: Archduke Franz Ferdinand assassinated. World War One begins. Egypt becomes British protectorate.	James Joyce, *The Dubliners*. Ezra Pound, *Des Imagistes*.

Year	Age	Life
1914–1918		Marie organizes 20 mobile X-ray cars and 200 radiological posts to treat wounded soldiers. Trains radiological staff at the Radium Institute. Irène works alongside her mother and alone at the front as a radiological worker.
1920	53	Marie meets Marie Mattingly Meloney. The Curie Foundation is started with a grant from Henri de Rothschild.
1921	54	Travels to America to receive gram of radium purchased with $100,000 raised by the women of America.
1922	55	Marie becomes member of the League of Nations' International Commission on Intellectual Cooperation. Has first of four cataract operations. She is elected to the Academy of Medicine.
1925	58	Irène defends her dissertation on the alpha rays of polonium.
1926	59	Irène marries Frédéric Joliot.
1929	62	Marie makes second trip to America to collect a gram of radium for the Radium Institute in Poland.
1932	65	Radium Institute inaugurated in Warsaw.
1934	67	January: Irène and Frédéric discover artificial radioactivity. July 4: Marie Curie dies.
1935		Irène and Frédéric Joliot-Curie share the Nobel Prize for chemistry.

Year	History	Culture
1916	Battle of the Somme. Battle of Jutland. Easter Rising in Ireland. Arab revolt against Ottoman Turks.	Guillaume Apollinaire, *Le poète assassiné*. G B Shaw, *Pygmalion*. Dada movement launched.
1919	Treaty of Versailles. Spartacist revolt in Germany. Poland, Hungary, Czechoslovakia, Estonia, Lithuania, and Latvia become republics. Comintern held in Moscow. In US, prohibition begins. Irish Civil War (until 1921).	Franz Kafka, *In the Penal Colony*. J M Keynes, *The Economic Consequences of the Peace*. The Bauhaus founded in Weimar. United Artists formed.
1920	IRA formed. First meeting of League of Nations.	Edith Wharton, *The Age of Innocence*.
1921	National Economic Policy in Soviet Union.	Sergei Prokofiev, *The Love of Three Oranges*. Luigi Pirandello, *Six Characters in Search of an Author*. Chaplin, *The Kid*.
1922	Soviet Union formed. Benito Mussolini's fascists march on Rome.	T S Eliot, *The Waste Land*. Joyce, *Ulysses*.
1925	Pact of Locarno. Chiang Kai-shek launches campaign to unify China. Discovery of ionosphere. Margaret Carlough, dial painter who worked with radium, sues her employer for damages to her health.	Erik Satie dies. F Scott Fitzgerald, *The Great Gatsby*. Kafka, *The Trial*. Adolf Hitler, *Mein Kampf* (Vol 1). Sergei Eisenstein, *Battleship Potemkin*. Television invented.
1926	Germany joins League of Nations. Antonio Gramsci imprisoned in Italy. France establishes Republic of Lebanon. Hirohito becomes emperor of Japan.	Kafka, *The Castle*. T E Lawrence, *The Seven Pillars of Wisdom*. A A Milne, *Winnie the Pooh*. Fritz Lang, *Metropolis*.
1929	Lateran Treaty. Yugoslavia kingdom under kings of Serbia. Wall Street crash. Young Plan for Germany.	William Faulkner, *The Sound and the Fury*. Robert Graves, *Good-bye to All That*. Ernest Hemingway, *A Farewell to Arms*. Erich Remarque, *All Quiet on the Western Front*.
1932	Kingdom of Saudi Arabia independent. Kingdom of Iraq independent. James Chadwick discovers neutron. First Autobahn opened.	Aldous Huxley, *Brave New World*. Bertolt Brecht, *The Mother*.
1934	Night of the Long Knives in Germany. Long March in China. Enrico Fermi sets off controlled nuclear reaction.	Dmitri Shostakovich, *The Lady Macbeth of the Mtsensk District*. Henry Miller, *Tropic of Cancer*.

Further Reading

PRIMARY SOURCES

Curie, Eve *Madame Curie* (London: 1938) the first and still the classic hagiography of Marie Curie. Contains many excerpts from letters lost in Warsaw during WWII.

Curie, Marie *Oeuvres de Marie Skłodowska Curie* (Warsaw: 1954) a useful reference that contains all of Marie Curie's published scientific papers in their original languages.

—— *Pierre Curie. With Autobiographical Notes* (New York: 1923) a concise remembrance of Pierre's life, with brief, occasionally revealing autobiography at the end. Curie allowed the autobiography to be published only in America during her lifetime.

—— *La Radiologie et la guerre* (Paris: 1921) a pragmatic post mortem on her wartime X-ray work.

—— *Recherches sur les substances radioactives* (Paris: 1903) her doctoral thesis, published immediately after she presented it as a cogent summary of the field.

—— *Marie–Irène Curie Correspondence*, ed. Ziegler (Paris: 1974) this collection of letters traces the development of the close relationship between Marie and Irène from when she was a child.

Joliot-Curie, Irène 'Marie Curie, ma mère' *Europe* 108 (1954) pp. 89–121: written for the 20th anniversary of her mother's death, it contains some detailed remembrances.

Rutherford, Ernest and Soddy, Frederick 'The Cause and Nature of Radioactivity' *Philosophical Magazine* 4 (1902) pp. 370–96: their landmark paper.

Soddy, Frederick, *Interpretation of Radium* (London: 1909) an enjoyable early popularization of radioactivity.

Strutt, R J *The Becquerel Rays and the Properties of Radium* (London: 1904) entertainingly written by the man who would become the fourth Lord Rayleigh. Contains experiments to try at home.

SECONDARY SOURCES

Abir-Am, Pnina G and Outram, Dorinda, eds. *Uneasy Careers and Intimate Lives: Women in Science 1789–1979* (New Brunswick, NJ: 1987).

Badash, Lawrence *Radioactivity in America: Growth and Decay of a Science* (Baltimore: 1979).

—— ed. *Rutherford and Boltwood: Letters on Radioactivity* (New Haven: 1969) letters across the Atlantic between the two physicists.

Boudia, Soraya 'The Curie Laboratory: Radioactivity and Metrology' *History and Technology*, 13 (1997) pp. 249–65.

—— *Marie Curie et son laboratoire* (Paris: 2001) the most up-to-date historiography on the role of measurements in the Curie laboratory.

Caulfield, Catherine *Multiple Exposures: Chronicles of the Radiation Age* (New York: 1989) snapshots from the history of radioactivity.

Clark, Claudia *Radium Girls: Women and Industrial Health Reform, 1910–1935* (Chapel Hill: 1997) a detailed history of the discovery and slow response to radium poisoning in America.

Crawford, Elizabeth *The Beginnings of the Nobel Institution: The Science Prizes, 1901–1915* (Cambridge: 1984).

Davis, J L 'The Research School of Marie Curie in the Paris Faculty, 1907–1914' *Annals of Science*, 52 (1995).

Forman, P et al 'Physics circa 1900: Personnel, Funding and Productivity of Academic Establishments' *Historical Studies in the Physical Sciences*, 5 (1975) pp. 1–185.

Hughes, Jeff, 'The French Connection: The Joliot-Curies and Nuclear Research in Paris, 1925–1933' *History and Technology*, 13 (1997) pp. 325–43.

Keller, Alex *The Infancy of Atomic Physics* (Oxford: 1983) a witty introduction to physics in Europe and America at the turn of the 20th century.

Malley, Marjorie 'The Discovery of Atomic Transmutation: Scientific Styles and Philosophies in France and Britain' *Isis*, 70 (1979) pp. 213–23

Marbo, Camille *À travers deux siècles 1883–1967* (Paris: 1968) the breezy memoir of Marguerite Borel, published under a pseudonym, including memories of Marie Curie during the Langevin scandal.

Paul, Henry *From Knowledge to Power: The Rise of the French Science Empire in France, 1860–1939* (Cambridge: 1985) an excellent history of institutional changes in the French scientific establishment.

Pestre, Dominique, 'The Moral and Political Economy of French Scientists in the First Half of the 20th Century' *History and Technology*, 13 (1997) pp. 241–8.

Pflaum, Rosalynd *Grand Obsession: Madame Curie and Her World* (New York: 1989) a biography of Marie with substantial material on Irène and Frédéric Joliot-Curie.

Pinault, Michel, 'The Joliot-Curies: Science, Politics, Networks' *History and Technology*, 13 (1997) pp. 307–24.

Pycior, Helena, 'Reaping the Benefits of Collaboration While Avoiding its Pitfalls: Marie Curie's Rise to Scientific Prominence' *Social Studies of Science*, 23 (1993) pp. 301–23.

Quinn, Susan *Marie Curie: A Life* (London: 1995) the most comprehensive English-language biography available, incorporating extensive primary source material and a lengthy treatment of the Langevin scandal.

Rayner-Canham, Marlene and Geoffrey, *A Devotion to Their Science: Pioneer Women of Radioactivity* (Quebec: 1997) a valuable and readable anthology of biographies of lesser-known women scientists such as Ellen Gleditsch, May Sybil Leslie, and Lise Meitner.

Reid, Robert *Marie Curie* (London: 1974) sharply written biography that is now somewhat out of date.

Romer, Alfred, *Radiochemistry and the Discovery of Isotopes* (New York: 1964) a useful collection of original papers on radioactivity by Becquerel, Rutherford, Soddy, and the Curies.

Roqué, Xavier, 'Marie Curie and the Radium Industry: A Preliminary Sketch' *History and Technology*, 13 (1997) pp. 267–91.

Walker, J Samuel *Permissible Dose: A History of Radiation Protection in the Twentieth Century* (Berkeley CA: 2000) detailed history of the development of industrial and medical standards for radiation protection in America, written by the historian of the United States Nuclear Regulatory Commission.

Wilson, David, *Rutherford: Simple Genius* (Cambridge MA: 1983) the authoritative and eminently readable biography.

Picture Sources

The author and publisher wish to express their thanks to the following sources of illustrative material and/or permission to reproduce it:

Ann Ronan Picture Library: pp. iii, vi, 2, 3, 7, 15, 17, 23, 27, 29, 41, 46, 50, 56, 61, 74, 79, 95, 102, 107, 110, 111, 125, 126, 135; Association Curie et Joliot-Curie: pp. 8, 21, 23, 50, 76, 82, 83, 99, 116, 118, 120, 128, 149; Science Museum, London / Heritage Image Partnership: pp. 11, 131; Topham Picturepoint: pp. 35, 121; Hulton-Deutsch Collection / Corbis: p. 85

Index